BRITAIN AT WAR

CLASSIC, RARE AND UNSEEN

BRITAIN AT WAR
CLASSIC, RARE AND UNSEEN

MAUREEN HILL

PHOTOGRAPHS FROM THE
Daily Mail

Trans
Atlantic
Press

This edition published by Transatlantic Press in 2009

Transatlantic Press
38 Copthorne Road
Croxley Green
Hertfordshire, WD3 4AQ, UK

CONTENTS

Britain's darkest and finest hour

This book deals with many facets of Britain at war, building up a collage of images to give a comprehensive picture of what the country looked like, what the people experienced and how they responded to what was a time of great individual and national trauma.

The photographs, restored to original condition, are drawn from the vast archive of the Daily Mail. Some were taken to accompany the news stories of the day; some to accompany morale-boosting features; others are obvious propaganda. A few were published at the time; some never got past the censor and others had instructions in the censor's blue pencil about what had to be blanked or cropped out, and what details the accompanying captions could tell, or not tell. Individually, each photograph tells a story and many in sequence form a compelling narrative. In addition the scribbled notes and typed captions on the rear of each photograph tell many interesting, fascinating, funny and tragic tales to add to the visual images.

These notes and captions have often found their way into the captions in this book, wholly or in part. The way in which they are written gives a vivid idea of the viewpoint at the time and often gives a strong sense of immediacy to the photographs they accompanied. Where this material has been used it appears in quotation marks. Sometimes a date has been added in brackets to indicate what 'today' or 'yesterday' meant in the original caption.

Each of the nine chapters opens with an overview of the topic but the whole book gives a comprehensive insight into the war, its opening, progress and the landmarks towards a British and Allied victory. The book is essentially a collage of Britain at war, the 'Home Front', presenting a detailed view in words and pictures of what everyday life was like for those in Britain during the war.

Men's lives are portrayed principally in the 'In Uniform' chapter, as it was they who formed the bulk of the armed forces and the whole of the combat force. In 'Women in the Workforce' there is a focus on women's contribution to the war effort. And the experiences and contributions of children are detailed in 'A Wartime Childhood'. However, these chapters are not alone in cataloguing the lives and experiences of the population of Britain under the greatest threat to their way of life in a millennium.

The whole book, through its memorable photographs and its detailed text, evokes a picture of people's daily experience and amazing courage under pressure. It is a testament to the spirit and hardwork of the British people and the support they gained from their Allies in what was Britain's darkest and its finest hour.

CHAPTER ONE

War is declared

At the end of September 1938, Prime Minister Neville Chamberlain had negotiated a peace deal in Munich with Adolf Hitler, whose annexation of the Sudetenland area of Czechoslovakia had sparked an international crisis. Just 20 years since the end of the 'Great War' there was little appetite for another conflict with Germany that would embroil vast tracts of Europe. Thus, Chamberlain agreed that those parts of Sudentenland occupied by ethnic Germans could become part of German territory. On return from the talks in Munich he declared, 'I believe it to be peace in our time.'

However, this appeasement policy became increasingly futile and, following Germany's refusal to conform to an ultimatum to withdraw from the Polish territory it had invaded on 1st September 1939, the British people expected the worst. When Chamberlain broadcast to the nation at 11.15 a.m. on 3rd September it was to proclaim that 'this country is now at war with Germany'.

Waiting for
the news

RIGHT: As it became clear that war was a likely consequence of Germany's refusal to withdraw from Poland, people gathered at Downing Street. Here police hold back the crowd on the morning of 3rd September.

BELOW LEFT: The Town Clerk reads the Royal Proclamation calling on all men up to the age of 36 to register for military service.

BELOW RIGHT: Soon after the declaration of war an air-raid warning sounded and people rushed for shelter.

OPPOSITE PAGE MIDDLE: Crowds in Downing Street on the morning of 3rd September as the declaration of war is made.

OPPOSITE PAGE BELOW: On 2nd September people had gathered in the streets around the Houses of Parliament to hear news of Prime Minister Chamberlain's speech to the Commons in which he was expected to deliver an ultimatum to Germany to withdraw from Polish territory. When he failed to do so the derision from MPs forced the Cabinet into late-night talks, from which discussions emerged a resolve to demand the withdrawal at 9.00 a.m. the following day, with an 11.00 a.m. deadline for compliance.

The opening moves

Following the declaration of war, Britain was swift to mobilise its military and by the second week in September, the British Expeditionary Force (BEF) had crossed the Channel to meet up with French forces. Together these troops moved to defend the Belgian border. The BEF was composed of regular and reserve soldiers; they were well trained but poorly equipped as a result of the paring back on defence spending in the 1920s and 1930s. This policy developed from the tacit belief, following the end of the Great War, the 'war to end all wars', that no country in Europe would ever wish a return to the wholesale salughter and carnage that war had caused.

OPPOSITE PAGE TOP: Even before war was declared the evacuation of children and vulnerable adults had started. These mothers are locked behind the platform gates at Waterloo Station, waving tearful farewells to their children boarding trains to safe areas.

OPPOSITE PAGE BELOW: Americans holidaying or living in Britain gather at the United States Line in Haymarket on 4th September to book their passage home.

LEFT ABOVE: On the same day that the Americans started leaving, the German Embassy in Carlton Terrace moved out.

LEFT MIDDLE: Demonstrating the special screen to be fitted to streetlamps in the blackout.

LEFT BELOW: Photographed on 6th October 1939, this message was typical of the support that the decision to declare war on Germany had engendered in the country.

A *place of safety*

The threat and fear of aerial bombardment, first seen in the First World War and developed by the Germans in the Spanish Civil War, led to a mass evacuation of children, young mothers, pregnant women and vulnerable adults from the major cities to safe areas.

Such an evacuation was a huge logistical undertaking which was accomplished relatively smoothly. Nevertheless, the human cost of the project, for those evacuated, those left behind in the cities, and those that housed the evacuees, was significant, emotionally, practically and socially.

OPPOSITE PAGE: A kindly policeman helps a London youngster on to an evacuation train.

OPPOSITE PAGE INSET LEFT: A soldier carries a sleeping child to the train.

OPPOSITE PAGE INSET RIGHT: Carrying their gas masks in cases and wearing luggage labels to help identify them, this group of children from the Hugh Myddelton School in Clerkenwell were part of the first wave of evacuees who left London on the day Hitler invaded Poland, 1st September, 1939.

ABOVE: Smiling children wave as they begin their evacuation to the south-east coast in June 1940 during the Battle of Britain.

RIGHT: Mother and the baby of the family bid farewell to big sister who is off with her schoolmates on a train bound for Yorkshire.

DANGER!

There will be surprise POISON GAS ATTACKS
during Richmond's Poison Gas Week, June 15 - 20

DON'T ASK!   CARRY YOUR MASK.

The 'phoney' war

Following the dispatch of the British Expeditionary Force, the mass evacuation of children and the practice drills in using gas masks and air-raid shelters, very little happened on either the fighting front or the home front. The term 'phoney war' was coined to reflect the fact that neither the Allies nor the Germans took any major initiatives. The BEF dug in with their allies in trenches in France during the winter of 1939–40. And no bombing raids on Britain had taken place, causing evacuees to drift back to their homes in the cities. Only at sea were there any sustained attacks by the Germans, who used their U-boats and magnetic mines to threaten the British merchant fleet and challenge the Royal Navy.

ABOVE: Richmond Council give notice of 'surprise' practice poison gas attacks.

RIGHT: A young couple walk hand in hand down a London street in the first month of the war.

OPPOSITE PAGE: During the months leading up to war 38 million gas masks were issued – one for everyone in the country. Although it was an offence not to carry your gas mask at all times many were forgotten, ending up as lost property, as this photograph of Baker Street Lost Property Office bears witness.

OPPOSITE PAGE INSET: Workmen sticking paper trellising on to a shop window to minimise damage from flying glass when the expected bombing came.

Protecting London's monuments

OPPOSITE PAGE ABOVE: Part of the preparations in anticipation of aerial bombardment was that many of the great civic statues and landmarks had to be protected. The civic landscape of many towns and cities changed, and the boarded-up statue of Eros and the 'Dig for Victory' banner are early signs of war in this picture of Piccadilly Circus.

OPPOSITE PAGE BELOW: Workmen erecting a protective cover over the statue of Eros at Piccadilly Circus in October 1939.

RIGHT TOP: This structure covers the equestrian statue of Charles I. Trafalgar Square, with the National Gallery, and the lions sitting boldly on their plinths, can be seen in the background.

RIGHT BELOW: Work in progress: the half-finished structure to protect the King Charles I statue. The timber-framed construction, filled with sandbags and faced with corrugated iron, cost £320.

Recruiting a fighting force

The 'phoney' war came to an abrupt end on 9th April 1940 when Hitler invaded Denmark and Norway, swiftly followed by attacks on the Low Countries and then France. This blitzkrieg or 'lightning war' saw the defeat of Allied troops. At Trondheim in Norway, 2000 German soldiers trained in winter warfare forced the withdrawal of a 13,000-strong Allied force. But, perhaps most famously, the blitzkrieg caused the evacuation of troops of the British Expeditionary Force and their allies from the beaches of Dunkirk in northern France between 28th May and 3rd June. Following the German occupation of most of Holland, Belgium and Luxembourg, and a large part of France, British

and French troops were pushed into a small pocket on the coast around Dunkirk. Operation Dynamo, as the rescue mission was codenamed, was expected at best to rescue 50,000 troops – in the event 338, 226 men were saved.

ABOVE: 'The first batch of men aged 22 but not yet 23 reported at various military centres today (15th January 1940) for training.' An act introducing conscription into the military had been passed in May 1939.

ABOVE INSET: Soon after the evacuation from Dunkirk, on 22nd June 1940, 30,000 men registered for military service at labour exchanges throughout the country.

OPPOSITE PAGE TOP: Just days before war is declared, call-up notices are being prepared for those who will become liable for military service on 15th September.

OPPOSITE PAGE MIDDLE: Troops line the beaches near Dunkirk, waiting to be evacuated back to Britain.

OPPOSITE PAGE BELOW RIGHT: Like this pair, men born in 1911, aged 28 in June 1940, were required to sign up for military service.

OPPOSITE PAGE BELOW LEFT: Sombre looking 36-year-old men sign on in January 1941.

Defenders for the home front

LEFT: Charles Remnant calls for volunteers to join the 'Citizen's Army' at a meeting held on Tooting Bec Common.

BELOW: The Citizen's Army hold their first parade on Tooting Bec Common, dressed in civilian clothes and 'armed' with sticks and umbrellas. It was intended as a defence force in the event of a German invasion.

OPPOSITE PAGE ABOVE: Local Defence Volunteers (LDV) on parade. The LDV was set up as Germany unleashed its blitzkrieg in Europe. In July 1940 the LDV changed its name to the Home Guard, which later became affectionately known as 'Dad's Army'. Many of those who joined up were older but had seen action in the Great War.

OPPOSITE PAGE BELOW: Local Defence Volunteers march at a parade ground in Balham. They are weaponless but some have LDV armbands and soldiers' caps.

A *new prime minister*

The spring 1940 blitzkrieg had significant effects, not only in continental Europe but also in Britain, where there was a profound political shift. Chamberlain resigned his premiership when he failed to prevent the German occupation of Norway, Denmark, Holland, Belgium and Luxembourg. On 10th May, Winston Churchill took over as prime minister at the head of a coalition government.

RIGHT: Just as the nation was pondering the consequences of the withdrawal from Dunkirk, Italy declared war on Britain on 10th June 1940. The Italian community, many of whom had been settled in Britain for years, responded to a number of anti-Italian demonstrations by removing any Italian symbols and by making clear, as here, their alliegance to Britain.

BELOW LEFT: Treasures from the National Gallery were evacuated to a disused slate mine in North Wales.

BELOW RIGHT: A Soho barber's shop removes the shop sign with its Italian language banner.

OPPOSITE PAGE TOP: These crowds gathered in front of an Italian café in Soho where windows had been smashed the night before in an anti-Italian demonstration.

OPPOSITE PAGE BELOW: Vapour trails from over 100 enemy aircraft captured on camera while making a vain daylight attempt to reach London during the Battle of Britain.

Bringing down the raiders

ABOVE: 'A Nazi 'plane attempting to pierce defences in a London area was shot down and crashed on this house. The woman occupant was sheltering in the passage and escaped unhurt.'

LEFT: Workmen clear up the rubble and make safe these houses in Yorkshire damaged by a raid in May 1940.

OPPOSITE PAGE TOP: A barrage balloon shot down by Luftwaffe fighters burns in the sky above Dover Castle.

OPPOSITE PAGE INSET: In June 1940, shortly after Churchill had told the nation that the Battle of Britain was about to begin, this school was damaged in a bombing raid.

175 GR
(and more) **Half F**
DOWN

MORE than 175 German 'planes and at least 350 airmen were shot down in the morning and afternoon attacks on London yesterday.

The R.A.F. lost 30 machines and 20 airmen.

In addition, German losses include :

18
on Saturday

Million

350
175

HITLER'S raids y the most sha

The Air between 350 a were launched London and sou

The Battle of Britain

Churchill turned the defeat at Dunkirk into a victory of the British spirit. Eight hundred civilian vessels joined 222 naval ships in Operation Dynamo to rescue the troops from the French beaches, but they could not bring off the military hardware that the British Expeditionary Force had taken with it. Britain faced the possibility of a German invasion and blitzkrieg with an army starved of weapons.

Hitler set the date of 15th September for a seaborne invasion of Britain. Operation Sea Lion was the codename for the invasion, and in order for troop ships to land unharried by air attack, the Luftwaffe needed to destroy the RAF's capability to mount a defence. So began the 'Battle of Britain'. For much of the summer of 1940 the skies over southern England and continental Europe were witness to dogfights between British and German planes. By the date set for the invasion the RAF had lost 915 planes, the Luftwaffe 1733; the failure to cripple Britain's air defences meant the invasion was called off.

ABOVE: A Luftwaffe plane plummets to the ground, shot down during a air battle with Spitfires in August 1940.

ABOVE INSET: During the Battle of Britain newspapers kept a running tally of the planes and airmen lost on both sides.

OPPOSITE PAGE TOP LEFT: Shot down in an air raid over Croydon, this wreckage is all that remains of a Messerschmitt 110 fighter-bomber which crashed at Bridgeham Farm near Horley in Surrey.

OPPOSITE PAGE TOP RIGHT: Another plane shot down by Spitfires in August 1940 – sometimes termed 'Spitfire Summer'. This one crashed in flames and Auxiliary Fire Service men put the fire out.

OPPOSITE PAGE BELOW: Vapour trails from a Spitfire patrol. The planes patrolled night and day, 'circling up high, ready to pounce on enemy raiders'.

'So much owed by so many'

The skill and bravery of the pilots and aircrew in the Battle of Britain saved the country from invasion and the sentiment of Churchill's testament to them – 'never in the field of human conflict was so much owed by so many to so few' – was shared by the nation. The focus on the air war in the summer of 1940 also bought time for the army to re-group and begin to re-arm. On 1st January 1940 two million men between the ages of 20 and 27 had been called up and most were still undergoing training while the retreat from France was taking place. Conscription for military service extended throughout the war to include adult men up to the age of 50, and in 1941 all women between the ages of 20 and 30 without carer responsibilities. Not everyone was expected to go into the fighting forces; many were sent to do essential war work in factories or administration, and from 1943 the 'Bevin Boys' were conscripted into the coal mines.

OPPOSITE PAGE TOP: Bullet holes from a Spitfire's machine guns can be seen peppering this plane's swastika symbol.

OPPOSITE PAGE INSET: The wreckage of this plane, brought down by anti-aircraft fire, was strewn across a railway line in south-east England.

OPPOSITE PAGE BELOW: Closely guarded by soldiers, this Luftwaffe fighter plane's good condition would reveal useful information about enemy aircraft design.

LEFT: 'The pilot of this Messerschmitt 109 fighter claimed three victories. Each of the white bars on the tail denotes one. The pilot was out to get his fourth on Saturday, but he met his match over south-east England. His squadron's crest carried the motto "Gott Strafe England."'

BELOW: As civilian sightseers gather the military stand guard over this Messerschmitt 109 shot down in raids over Ramsgate.

Messerschmitt reaches Parliament

OPPOSITE PAGE ABOVE: Shot down as a result of a dogfight over the south-east of England, the pilot of this plane was taken into custody by the Home Guard. The aircraft remained in the field and the farmer carried on his peaceful work of rounding up the sheep.

OPPOSITE PAGE BELOW: Polish airmen, many of whom were stationed in Brtiain during the war, shot down this Junkers 88. The plane landed in a cornfield near the north-east coast. Some of its crew were injured, but all were taken prisoner.

ABOVE: 'Not how the pilot of this Messerschmitt would have liked to have seen Westminster. A German machine being taken through London on its way to the scrap heap today.'

BELOW: The man on the ladder is searching a tree for bits of the Junkers 88 which crashed in the north-east cornfield.

Facing up to the Blitz

One year on from the declaration of war, life for everyone in the country had changed. Families were fragmented, with many men away on military service and children evacuated to safe areas. Women, banned from many workplaces before the war, found themselves to be vital to the production of munitions. And shortages and rationing of food, clothing and household items made everyday life a struggle. Over and above these concerns there was a constant fear of invasion and aerial bombardment. In August 1940 when bombing raids began on British cities and towns it came as no surprise.

London was attacked on 25th August. Following a retaliatory raid on Berlin, 21 British towns and cities were targeted by the Luftwaffe on 27th August. Then on 7th September London suffered the first in a series of raids which became known as the London Blitz. The Germans widened their targets to include cities and towns such as Coventry, Southampton, Liverpool, Glasgow, Bristol and Birmingham. By November 1940, the Blitz had arrived across Britain.

BELOW LEFT: An RAF corporal inspects bullet holes in the tail of a German plane on a reconnaisance flight shot down near Dalkeith, Scotland.

BELOW RIGHT: The pilot of the plane shot down near Dalkeith survived unhurt, but two of the crew died.

OPPOSITE PAGE TOP: This German plane crashed nose-first into a field near the coast of north-east England.

OPPOSITE PAGE BELOW: A Messerschmitt 109 shot down by British fighters after it had crossed into British territory over south-east England.

CHAPTER TWO

The Blitz

The Blitz is probably the most vivid image associated with life on the home front during the Second World War. The idea that civilians were vulnerable to military attack from the air was relatively new; there had been attempts to use zeppelins to bomb London in the First World War, attacks that were largely unsuccessful and infrequent. By 1939, aircraft technology had seen major developments, and the Luftwaffe gained experience of mounting coordinated bombing runs during the Spanish Civil War, most notably at Guernica in 1937. For British civilians, the real Blitz covered a nine month period from September 1940 until May 1941, during which time 43,000 lost their lives. By June 1941 the Luftwaffe were needed to support the fighting on the Eastern Front that had opened with Germany's declaration of war on its former ally, the Soviet Union. However, this did not mean that Britain was safe from aerial attack.

First strikes

London was the focus for most Blitz attacks and the 7th September 1940 marked the first in a series of raids on the capital that continued for the next 56 days. At first, the Germans mounted sorties day and night but losses were large and after a week the Luftwaffe switched most of their operations to take place under cover of darkness. Up to the 15th September the bombing was part of Hitler's invasion strategy, which necessitated the destruction of RAF capability to attack German troop ships landing on the British coast.

OPPOSITE PAGE ABOVE: A downed fighter-bomber lies almost intact in this London street.

OPPOSITE PAGE BELOW: The wreckage of a tram car damaged in a daylight raid in Blackfriars Road.

LEFT ABOVE: A London trolley-bus, wrecked during a raid.

LEFT BELOW: RAF officers survey the wreckage of the engine and propeller of a Dornier which was brought down near a London Station during a daylight raid.

Hitting London's heart

OPPOSITE PAGE ABOVE: An anti-aircraft battery in action at the height of a bombing raid on London.

OPPOSITE PAGE MIDDLE: One of London's most famous shopping areas, Burlington Arcade, hit during an attack in September 1940.

OPPOSITE PAGE BELOW: 'Piccadilly Circus. Hardly a pedestrian to be seen. Delayed action bombs in the vicinity caused this area to be closed to traffic.'

RIGHT: Firemen play their hoses on the National Bank in Oxford Street, hit during an early Blitz raid.

BELOW: The same raid also hit John Lewis's department store on the opposite corner.

Surveying the damage

ABOVE: Locals in a south-west London suburb shop as usual, despite the damage caused by German bombs in a raid the previous night.

LEFT: While the side of this house is blown away, on the first floor the kitchen range with its clock and horse statues on the mantel are untouched, and on the floor above the mirror has not even suffered a crack.

OPPOSITE PAGE ABOVE: Grose's sports shop in New Bridge Street was hit in December 1940; the blast blew bicycles upwards into the rafters.

OPPOSITE PAGE LEFT MIDDLE: Civilians survey the damage to the Ring Sports Stadium at Blackfriars, wrecked by bombs in October 1940.

OPPOSITE PAGE LEFT BELOW: Rescuing a valuable painting from the debris of a bombed-out building.

OPPOSITE PAGE BELOW RIGHT: An Eton boy moves his belongings after stray bombs dropped on the school in December 1940.

Attacking public morale

When Hitler's plans for a seaborne invasion on 15th September 1940 were thwarted by the skill and courage of the RAF, Luftwaffe bombing campaigns found a new rationale. The intention was that the death and destruction caused by bombing would severely damage morale, with the consequence that the population would urge the government to sue for peace; it was a policy adopted later in the war by the Allies. Thus, German attacks on London were designed as a symbolic blow to the capital of Britain, the Commonwealth and the Empire, while also seeking to damage the administrative heart of the country and disrupt the government's capacity to conduct the war effectively.

OPPOSITE PAGE ABOVE: A watchful guard stands amid the wreckage in Cloister Court within the Houses of Parliament; the damage came during a twelve-hour raid on London by 413 aircraft in December 1940.

OPPOSITE PAGE INSET: Fallen masonry lies on the terrace outside County Hall on the Thames embankment, after the building was bombed in September 1940.

OPPOSITE PAGE BELOW: Transport authorities had to deal with damage to the infrastructure as well as damage to vehicles. Here a railway bridge is wrecked.

RIGHT: Damage to this London bus was caused by falling masonry. Damage to London's buses became so severe that the authorities had to commandeer vehicles from the provinces to keep services running.

BELOW: Another damaged bus – this time hit by a bomb dropped during a raid on 11th September 1940.

Salvaging belongings

OPPOSITE PAGE ABOVE LEFT: Part of the ground floor of Whiteley's department store, Bayswater, that was severely damaged in a raid in October 1940.

OPPOSITE PAGE ABOVE RIGHT: This house in a terrace row was demolished when a German bomb dropped on it.

OPPOSITE PAGE BELOW: As they salvage what they can of their belongings from the wreckage of their home, these Londoners are offered a welome cup of tea by a Salvation Army worker.

LEFT: The occupant of this home, Mrs Mann, managed a lucky escape when a bomb dropped on the rear of her cottage in outer London as she slept in her bedroom.

BELOW: 'Mrs M. Robertson and her family removing articles from their wrecked house.'

Avoiding 'deep shelter mentality'

In London, Blitz casualties were high with 13,000 killed and 20,000 injured during September and October alone. However, the availability of deep shelters in the London Underground system kept numbers lower than might have been expected. Tube stations became Londoners preferred shelters; initially the government were averse to the system being used for this purpose, in the belief that it would seriously hamper the Underground's ability to function and that it would foster a 'deep shelter mentality' in which the population of the capital spent long periods of time below ground, fearful of air raids. However, public demand and the clear evidence that the city and its people could still function as normally as could be expected, changed the authorities' minds.

OPPOSITE PAGE ABOVE: Auxiliary Fire Service (AFS) men pump water from the Thames to fight fires caused by incendiary bombs.

OPPOSITE PAGE MIDDLE LEFT: Cobblestones, dislodged by the bombing, provide another hazard to transport.

OPPOSITE PAGE MIDDLE RIGHT: Operations board from the War Cabinet HQ under Storey's Gate from where Churchill and the cabinet would conduct the war during raids on London.

OPPOSITE PAGE BELOW: East Enders queue patiently to enter air-raid shelters.

ABOVE RIGHT: The roof of the District Line tunnel was damaged in a raid in October 1940 but trains continued to run.

RIGHT: Troops cross a temporary road bridge over London's largest bomb crater, at Bank tube station. The immense crater was caused by a direct hit on 11th January 1941 that killed at least fifty people. The censor gave permission for this picture to appear in the newspapers on condition that all of the crater was blacked out, and only the road bridge, with the troops crossing it, was shown.

Demolishing the danger

LEFT: A bomb-damaged office block is demolished to protect the public from the danger of falling masonry.

BELOW: Members of the Pioneer Corps rest and refresh themselves during a salvage and clear-up operation.

OPPOSITE PAGE ABOVE: A public meeting in March 1942 at which, despite the bombing and the privations of war, there were calls for a more active stance against Germany.

OPPOSITE PAGE INSET: Sisters from a London convent inspect the damage caused to their buildings which were used as an air-raid shelter.

OPPOSITE PAGE BELOW: Despite the bombing, the Union Jack flies defiantly.

The Fire of London

OPPOSITE PAGE: One of the most devastating raids, resulting in what came to be known as 'the Second Great Fire of London', occurred on 29th December 1940. More than 10,000 fire-bombs rained down on the city on a night when the River Thames was at its lowest and enemy aircraft had earlier in the evening hit the water mains. The 20,000 firemen struggling with the blaze were reinforced by soldiers and civilians. Here the Pioneer Corps clear up around Tower Hill after the raid – the Tower of London can be seen in the background.

RIGHT: Workers gather outside their blitzed premises following the raid.

BELOW INSET: The ruins of a once busy street in Aldermanbury, near the Guildhall.

BELOW: St Anne's Parochial School, Hatton Garden ablaze as firefighters struggle to bring the flames under control on 29th December 1940.

New Year 1941

OPPOSITE PAGE ABOVE: The Guildhall suffered severe damage during the raid. Here, wreckage of the roof beams lies in the Banqueting Hall. It was to take years of careful restoration work post-war to return the building to its former glory.

OPPOSITE PAGE BELOW LEFT: On New Year's Day 1941, the Lord Mayor of London toured the ruins, here inspecting the damage in the Guildhall.

OPPOSITE PAGE BELOW RIGHT: The Lord Mayor at Aldermanbury, where the Wren church of St Mary the Virgin had taken a direct hit during the raid.

BELOW: The medieval walls of the Guildhall survived the Fire of London but the wooden roof, that was not as old as the walls, burned, the debris falling into the building.

St. Clement Danes Church

NOTICE

This Church is dangerous, pending repairs, on account of falling pieces of brick and stone. The public are warned to keep away from the walls—those who enter, do so at their own risk, and must keep within the roped enclosure.

MORNING PRAYER & SERMON are held on Sunday Mornings at 11 a.m. in The Parish House, Portugal Street, near by.

History of the Church—Postcards etc., can be obtained from the Verger, 8, Clements Inn Passage.

THE SECRETARY OF THE PAROCHIAL CHURCH COUNCIL.

Smoking ruins

MAIN PICTURE: A lone emergency worker surveys the smoking ruins and debris in the street on the morning of the 30th December 1940.

OPPOSITE PAGE INSET: A view of the Guildhall Library, with books rescued from the 25,000-volume collection, much of which was lost.

LEFT INSET: The interior of the Wren-built church of St Bride's in Fleet Street was gutted in the fire.

ABOVE: A notice outside St Clement Danes Church reads as a testament to the fact that London carried on whatever the bombers might throw at it.

Aftermath of the fire

ABOVE: The Duke of Kent (front, middle), later killed while serving as a pilot in the RAF, inspects the damage a week after the fire Blitz on London on 29th December 1940.

LEFT: Royal Engineers demolish unsafe masonry on 3rd January 1941.

OPPOSITE PAGE TOP LEFT: Even after the raid the public were not safe from explosions. A photographer captures the moment a delayed action bomb went off on the outskirts of London.

OPPOSITE PAGE TOP RIGHT: On 3rd January 1941 a series of pictures were taken from the dome of St Paul's Cathedral surveying the damage from the raid.

OPPOSITE PAGE BELOW: The City a year on from the Great Fire.

St Paul's untouched amid the ruins

OPPOSITE PAGE ABOVE LEFT: The City from the west of the Old Bailey – Justice with her scales is just visible.

OPPOSITE PAGE TOP RIGHT: Taken a week after the Fire of London, this picture of St Paul's shows the ruins around the cathedral are still smouldering. One of the most powerful images of the war was captured on the night of the 29th December – it shows St Paul's standing untouched amid the flames and smoke. It was taken from the roof of the Daily Mail building by photographer Herbert Mason.

OPPOSITE PAGE BELOW: Although St Paul's escaped damage during the Great Fire, it was hit by German bombs during the course of the war. This crater in the north transept was made by a bomb dropped during a raid in April 1941.

BELOW: A view of the north side of St Paul's as the clear-up continues around the great building.

Legacy of the bombing

Following the Fire of London raid, the capital suffered almost nightly bombing until May 1941. During the night of 11th May over 500 Luftwaffe planes dropped hundreds of high explosive bombs and tens of thousands of incendiary devices. Many important London landmarks were damaged that night, including the chamber of the House of Commons and Big Ben. This was the last great bombing raid on London, but one of the legacies of the months of sustained bombing, a legacy that lasted for many years, was the fear of the attackers returning.

OPPOSITE PAGE: 'A postman tries to deliver letters in historic Watling Street, Roman highway, in the city of London, after the latest indiscriminate Nazi raid.'

RIGHT ABOVE: The Blitzed area around St Paul's, pictured in May 1943.

RIGHT MIDDLE: Thurston's, home of billiards, and the Automobile Association's HQ, that stand side-by-side in Leicester Square, were damaged when a bomb dropped on the area in October 1940.

BELOW: A London family made homeless by the bombing sit in the street awaiting a removal van.

Bombed out of home

LEFT: A fire hose lies amid the debris in Fetter Lane on 12th May 1941 after what was, in effect, the last significant raid on London in the Blitz.

BELOW: Families sit outside their homes in a South London street with all they have managed to save, following the bombing of the area.

OPPOSITE PAGE ABOVE: Salvaging belongings, while a nun offers some comfort.

OPPOSITE PAGE BELOW: Moving out of a bombed-out home in Hendon.

Blitz routines

In the closing months of 1940, life for most Londoners became a relentless routine of making for the shelters almost as soon as dusk fell, to sleep or doze through the night, listening to wave after wave of Luftwaffe bombers targeting the city. Morning meant emerging from the shelter to face the extent of the damage. Days were spent at work, or clearing up the remains of bombed homes and workplaces, or trying to look after a family at home or, for those made homeless, in temporary accommodation in public buildings such as schools and church halls.

RIGHT ABOVE: Residents of the Guinness Trust Buildings in the Kings Road, Chelsea, salvage their belongings.

RIGHT BELOW: Although their doorway was wrecked, this family escaped uninjured when bombs fell less than 200-yards from their cottage in the Ashdown Forest.

BELOW: Miss Olive Unwin lost her home and her wedding trousseau when a bomb destroyed her Cambridgeshire home.

OPPOSITE PAGE ABOVE: A member of the Pioneer Corps, wearing his tin hat, works to clear up bomb damage. Many of the Pioneer Corps were recruited from the ranks of the the unemployed and their task was to help with salvage and clearance operations.

OPPOSITE PAGE BELOW: A London family hitches a ride on the tailboard of the removal van taking their belongings to a place of safety.

Raids on Southampton

BELOW: Dealing with people made homeless by raids on Southampton in December 1940.

FAR LEFT: This family, made homeless when a bomb damaged their Westminster home in April 1941, are moving to a new billet in a '£100-a-week Park-Lane luxury flat.'

LEFT: Miss Muddle was rescued from beneath this door which fell on her when an enemy plane crashed near her home in Clacton.

OPPOSITE PAGE ABOVE: In May 1941, amid the bomb rubble, office workers enjoy a basin of soup provided by the American Food Convoys.

OPPOSITE PAGE BELOW: Homeless children queuing for a free hot bath, a service, with free soap and towels, provided by Lever Brothers.

Bombs on Buckingham Palace

Lowering public morale was a key aim in the German High Command's bombing strategy. And it proved to be a frightening experience for many, and affected everyone's life. Nevertheless, while every member of the population was touched in some way, they did not become demoralised. In fact, the constant attacks seemed to provoke the reverse effect to that intended – the sense of a nation pulling together, for bombs did not discriminate, no one, not even the King and Queen who remained in Buckingham Palace for the duration of the war, was spared the effects, or the fear.

OPPOSITE PAGE ABOVE: When, in September 1940, five bombs dropped in the vicinity of Buckingham Palace, this crater outside the gates was caused by one of them.

OPPOSITE PAGE BELOW: The North Lodge, next to Constitution Hill, received a direct hit in a raid in March 1941. A policeman died when one of the stone pillars fell on him.

ABOVE: Workmen labour to repair another area of damage just outside the Palace gates, caused by the five bombs dropped in September 1940.

LEFT: A policeman shows off some of the wreckage caused by the bomb that destroyed the Palace's North Lodge.

Services for the homeless

LEFT ABOVE: This vehicle provided a free clothes washing service for those displaced or made homeless by the bombing.

LEFT MIDDLE: Villagers in East Anglia gather round a crater made by a bomb that killed a pony and a cow.

LEFT BELOW: Following the destruction of the premises these office workers wait in the street for instructions. Behind them posters promote War Savings; by March 1942 Britain had spent £9050 million on the war – ordinary people's savings as well as their taxes had helped to pay the costs.

BELOW: A pet rabbit was discovered alive in the bomb debris after a raid in Cambridgeshire.

OPPOSITE PAGE ABOVE: The photographer captures the moment when a delayed action bomb startled these women.

OPPOSITE PAGE BELOW: Clacton Pier was damaged by a bomb in February 1940.

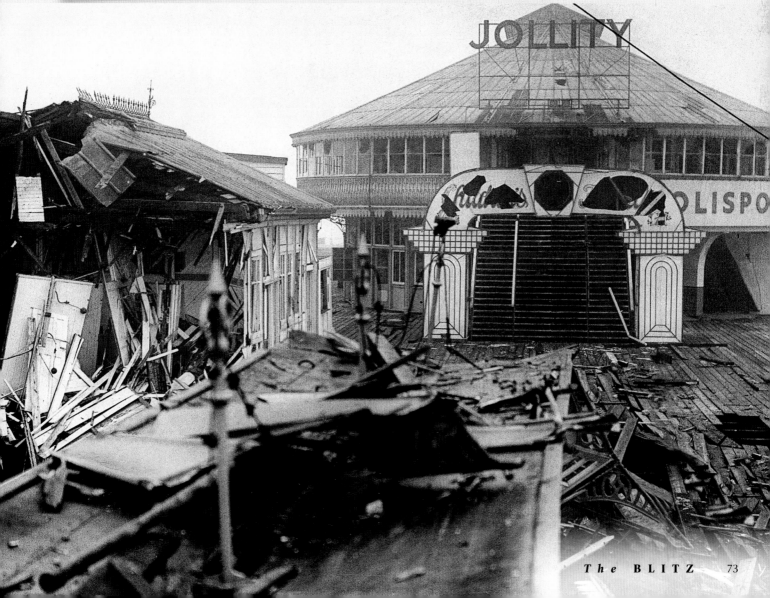

Lessons from Clacton

OPPOSITE PAGE ABOVE: In May 1940, before the Blitz, a Luftwaffe plane laying mines in the North Sea crashed in Clacton and the mines onboard blew up. Here, ARP Control Staff from various London Boroughs visit the scene to hear of Clacton ARP's experience with such a major incident.

OPPOSITE PAGE BELOW LEFT AND RIGHT: Clearing up in the streets of terraced housing that surrounded the city of Norwich. The historic city centre suffered significant damage when targeted as part of the 'Baedeker Raids'.

ABOVE: A bombing raid on Brighton in August 1943 damaged the railway bridge, exposing the railway lines and revealing a view of the church in the background.

LEFT: Soldiers looking for salvage items and materials from the homes damaged by the mine-laying plane that crashed in Clacton.

Plymouth a prime target

RIGHT: As home to Devonport, Britain's major naval base, Plymouth was a prime Luftwaffe target as German High Command sought to gain domination in the Atlantic. As a consequence, the city was hit by almost 60 air raids. Here, sailors help with the clear-up after three successive nights of raids in April 1941.

BELOW LEFT: A view across the city at the end of 1941, with the ruined Guildhall in the foreground and the damage in the surrounding area.

BELOW RIGHT: This rubble is all that remains of the Royal Sailors' Rest, founded by Dame Agnes Weston. In the background is the needle of the Devonport Column

OPPOSITE PAGE ABOVE: The Dean of St Peter's Church in Plymouth reflects on the ruins of the bombed-out church.

OPPOSITE PAGE BELOW: Hosing down business premises after a raid.

School hit in daylight

OPPOSITE PAGE ABOVE LEFT: An injured child is cared for by a nurse at Queen Mary's Hospital, Sidcup. She was injured when a bomb landed on Sandhurst Road School in Catford, killing 38 children.

OPPOSITE PAGE ABOVE RIGHT: Victims of 'bomb shock', these toddlers are being cared for at a convalescent home in Hertfordshire.

OPPOSITE PAGE MIDDLE RIGHT: Houses damaged when a mine-laying plane crashed in Clacton.

OPPOSITE PAGE BELOW LEFT: Mr and Mrs Calvert lost their eight-roomed house in the Clacton disaster.

OPPOSITE PAGE BELOW RIGHT: An injured man is led away from the the bomb scene in Sandhurst Road.

ABOVE: Disposing of one of the live mines that did not explode on impact in Clacton.

RIGHT: The scene at Sandhurst Road School in Catford as rescue workers strive to reach children and teachers.

Hospitals are bomb targets

LEFT: Mr E. Smith from the National Physical Laboratory searches the debris of this London hospital with an 'electric detector' for radium from damaged X-ray equipment.

BELOW: Salvaging whatever can be saved from the wards. Everything that could be saved and re-used was rescued, cleaned, mended or sent for recycling.

OPPOSITE PAGE ABOVE: Unfortunately, several casualties occurred when this hospital was bombed in November 1940.

OPPOSITE PAGE BELOW: A wrecked ward in the London Chest Hospital.

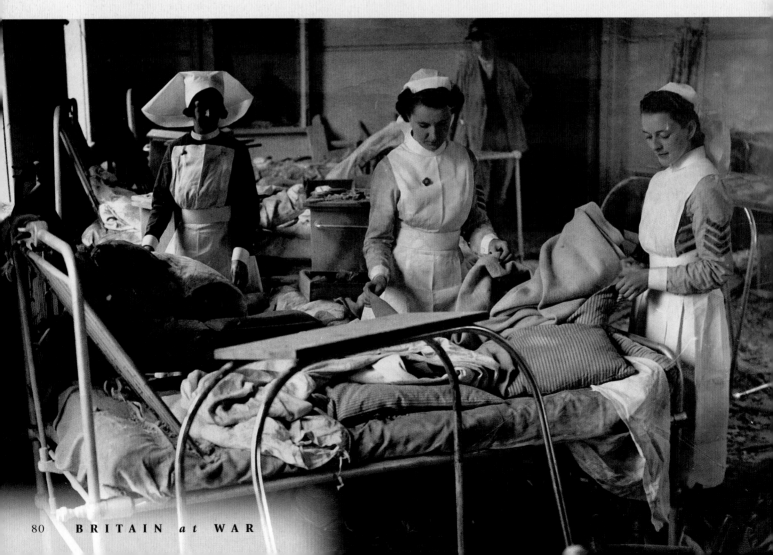

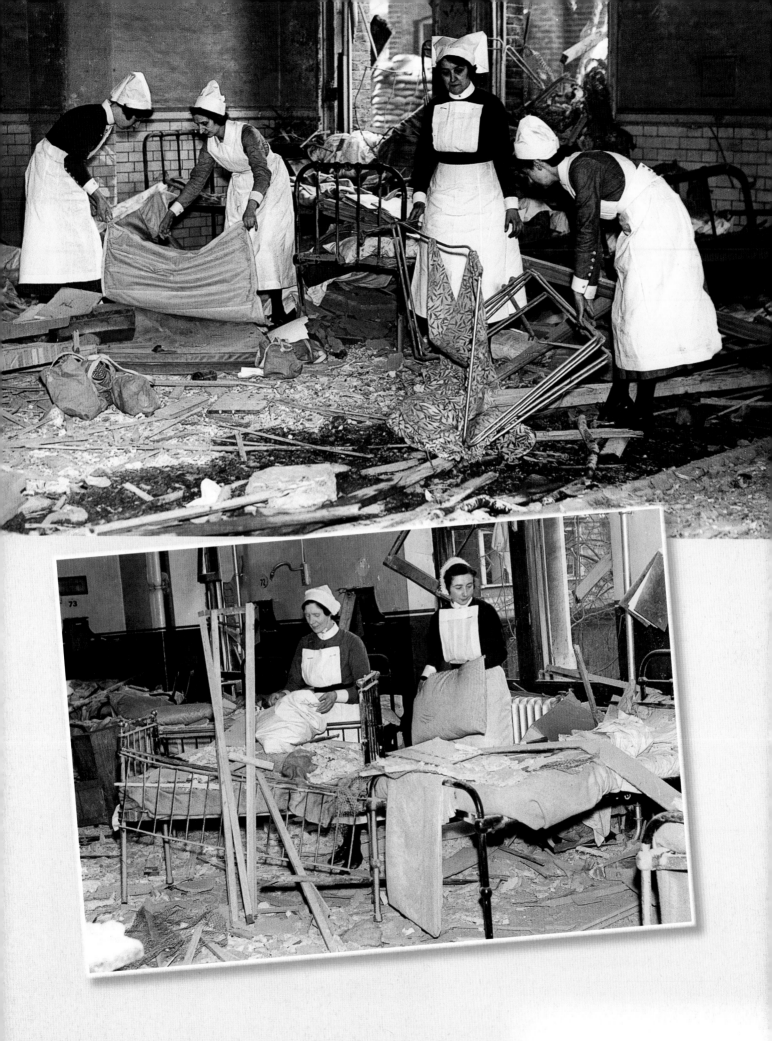

Nursing work

OPPOSITE PAGE ABOVE: Nurses clear up in one of four wards wrecked in this hospital, hit during an early raid in the Blitz.

OPPOSITE PAGE BELOW LEFT: A nurse salvages bedding from the rubble of one of six hospitals hit during a raid in March 1941.

OPPOSITE PAGE BELOW RIGHT: ATS plant poppies in memory of civilians killed during the war, on Remembrance Day 1940.

RIGHT: Nurses salvaging among the wreckage of their hospital, hit in March 1941.

BELOW RIGHT: A notice posted outside St Stephen's Hospital, Fulham, where three male wards were destroyed and several men killed, but all female patients were saved, rescued by nurses, who had been attending a dance; staff worked by torchlight, wearing evening dress.

BELOW LEFT: 8th April 1941. 'As usual a Hospital was one of the targets in last night's raid. Nurses salvaging in the debris of a London hospital for the aged and infirm.'

Coventry blitzed

A devastating attack on the ancient cathedral city of Coventry on 14th November 1940 was the first major raid on a town or city outside London. It marked a change in the tactics of the German High Command; not only were there to be attacks on the symbolic heart of the nation, but the destruction was to be spread throughout the country. The attack on Coventry was carried out by a squad of 500 bombers which dropped 500 tonnes of high explosives and 36,000 incendiaries in an attempt to set the city ablaze. The strategy was largely successful and although firecrews and emergency services worked tirelessly, by the morning Coventry's mediaeval cathedral was almost entirely reduced to rubble, along with around 50,000 buildings. A death toll of 568 civilians was reported.

OPPOSITE PAGE: Coventry Cathedral in November 1940 after the devastating raid on the fourteenth.

LEFT ABOVE: The burned-out interior of St Nicholas Church, Liverpool, which was hit by a number of incendiary bombs in a raid on 20th December 1940.

LEFT BELOW: A café and shops were wrecked when a bomb dropped on this unidentified north-east coastal town. People in the buildings were brought out when rescue workers dug a hole in order to access the basement.

Midlands raided

ABOVE: Amid the wreckage, the YMCA offer the bombed-out citizens of Coventry welcome cups of tea.

ABOVE INSET: Salvaging the contents of a home wrecked in a raid on Birmingham.

LEFT: MIDDLE: This was once a busy shopping street in Coventry.

LEFT BELOW: Less than 48 hours after the raid on 14th Novemebr 1940, the people of Coventry go about their business through the city's smouldering ruins.

OPPOSITE PAGE: On the night of 22nd November 1940, Birmingham was subjected to an 11-hour raid. As a major manufacturing centre the city was an obvious target. Transport and telephone systems were severely affected but it was damage to the water system which caused the most urgent problem – firefighters had to rely on pumping water from the canals or leave some fires to burn themselves out. Here the struggle continues to extinguish the fire in this factory.

Coventry's shopping centre

MAIN PICTURE: Coventry's main shopping area still smoulders on the 15th November 1940, following the previous night's 13-hour raid, which saw the Luftwaffe fly sortie after sortie to bomb the ancient city.

BELOW: The interior of a Dover church damaged by long-range German shells.

BELOW INSET: Mr and Mrs Dykes inspect damage to their home, following an air battle over the south-east coast during the Battle of Britain.

OPPOSITE PAGE BELOW: Damage to a shopping arcade in Birmingham.
.

Communal graves

ABOVE: A hundred and seventy-two victims from the raid on Coventry in November 1941 were buried in a communal grave.

ABOVE INSET: 'The twenty-six victims of the bombed village school were buried in a communal grave in Sussex today.' (Saturday, 3rd October 1942).

LEFT: Workmen in the foreground sort through the bomb debris for materials for re-use, while others carry out repairs on these houses in Cambridgeshire.

OPPOSITE PAGE: 'Stout wellingtons, tin hat and firm jaw - this lad sums up the resolve of a group of Londoners talking over last night's raid.'

OPPOSITE PAGE INSET: People move through the piles of bricks in what is left of the streets of Coventry.

The BLITZ 91

Trapped in a shelter

ABOVE: More than a hundred people were trapped in a public air-raid shelter underneath this furniture depository when three German planes attacked Southampton in August 1940. Burning debris blocked their exit. All were safely rescued with help from firefighters, seen here damping down the remains.

LEFT: Mrs Williams in the wreckage of her home, destroyed in a raid on Surrey. She and her baby sheltered in a cupboard under the stairs and were unhurt.

RIGHT: The ruins of a bombed church in Southampton.

BELOW: The Pioneer Corp work among the wreckage of a Midland town in November 1940.

BOTTOM: Rescue workers are quickly on the scene of an attack on a south-east town; by this time, March 1943, such towns were prone to frequent hit-and-run raids, earning the area the nickname of 'bombers' alley'.

Blitz on the industrial base

As well as raiding the symbolic heart of the nation, the industrial base of the country was targeted by the Luftwaffe in an attempt to destroy the means by which Britain could continue to prosecute the war. Birmingham, Sheffield, Manchester, Glasgow and other centres of aircraft, military vehicle, weapon and munitions production suffered devastating raids. So too did ports like Southampton, Bristol and Liverpool as the naval dockyards and navy and merchant ships were targeted.

BELOW AND BELOW RIGHT: Firefighters tackle fires set off during a raid on Manchester.

BOTTOM: Gunners from Cheshire's Inland Royal Artillery Unit rush to their gun at the sound of the alert.

OPPOSITE PAGE ABOVE: A view of the damage to buildings in Bosley Street, Manchester, after a raid at the beginning of January 1941.

OPPOSITE PAGE BELOW: Following a blaze in the next-door building Northcliffe house, Manchester offices of the *Daily Mail*, sustained damage [LEFT]. Decorative detail on the entrance on Deansgate was damaged [RIGHT] in the raid in June 1940.

Sheffield hit

BELOW INSET: The Sheffield Blitz, on 12th December 1940, left Sheffield United's Bramall Lane stand wrecked.

RIGHT: Old Trafford football ground was hit during raids on Manchester.

BELOW: The damage to Manchester's city centre after the raids just before Christmas 1940.

OPPOSITE PAGE ABOVE: Virtually every tram car in Sheffield was left with some degree of damage – 31 were totally destroyed.

OPPOSIT PAGE BELOW: Like Manchester, Liverpool was blitzed in the week before Christmas 1940. Here, rescuers sift through the wreckage of homes.

Liverpool's Christmas Blitz

OPPOSITE PAGE ABOVE: Troops assist in clearing the debris in Sheffield after a major raid on 12th December 1940. Only three days later the city was attacked again. This was a frequent pattern in the Germans' bombing strategy – the raiders returned after a brief respite, just enough time to begin the clear-up operation.

OPPOSITE PAGE BELOW AND THIS PAGE ABOVE: Liverpool and the Birkenhead area suffered two nights of heavy attack on 20th and 21st December 1940. More than 200 people were killed in these raids. These pictures were taken after demolition squads had worked to make the city safe.

ABOVE INSET: A bomb crater in the back yard of a house in the North Riding of Yorkshire.

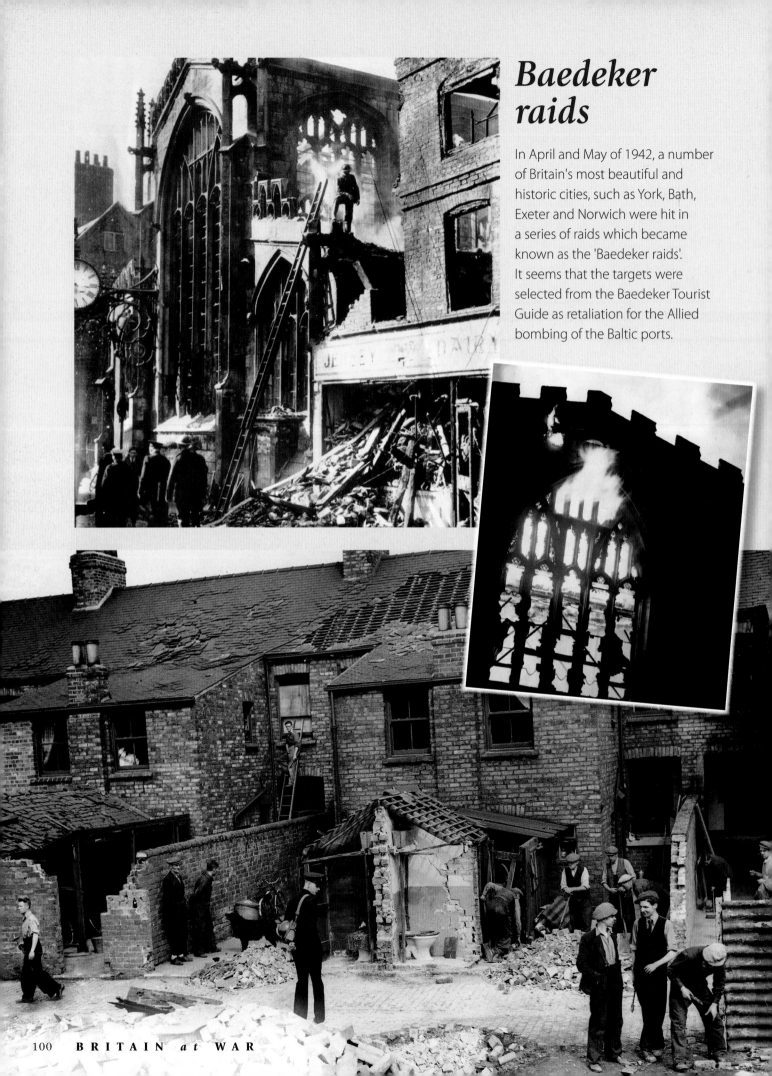

Baedeker raids

In April and May of 1942, a number of Britain's most beautiful and historic cities, such as York, Bath, Exeter and Norwich were hit in a series of raids which became known as the 'Baedeker raids'. It seems that the targets were selected from the Baedeker Tourist Guide as retaliation for the Allied bombing of the Baltic ports.

OPPOSITE PAGE ABOVE: A church in York after a Baedeker raid. Damage was severe in these provincial towns and cities as they had fewer air defences than other, more likely targets.

OPPOSITE PAGE INSET: York's 15th-century Guildhall in flames, after a raid in retribution for RAF attacks on Baltic ports.

OPPOSITE PAGE BELOW: Stray bombs demolished outhouses and brought slates from the roofs of these houses in a town in the North Riding of Yorkshire. Areas not designated as bomb targets were vulnerable to such random acts, as bombs fell accidently, or were jettisoned by bomber crews, or planes crash landed.

ABOVE: Middlesbrough Railway Station after a bombing raid in November 1942.

RIGHT: An air raid in Hull in July 1941 caused extensive damage in New Bridge Road, a residential district.

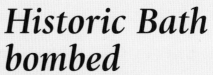

Historic Bath bombed

OPPOSITE PAGE ABOVE: The ruins of St Andrew's Church in Bath, gutted by fire after a Baedeker raid in April 1942.

OPPOSITE PAGE BELOW: A comic moment as Pioneer Corps come across a relic from the past in the rubble of bombed Bath.

ABOVE LEFT: 'The Luftwaffe have made yet another vicious "reprisal" raid on Bath. Swooping low in the moonlight, a demon Nazi plane dive-bombed and fired many of Bath's famous buildings for the second time, and sprayed the streets with machine-gun fire.
Photo shows: Searching for victims in the ruins of St John's Roman Catholic Church which received a direct hit. One of the priests was killed.'

ABOVE RIGHT: Bomb damage to one of Bath's beautiful Georgian Crescents.

LEFT: 'Thick grey dust covered the houses and roadway after the havoc caused in a Bath thoroughfare by Nazi raiders.'

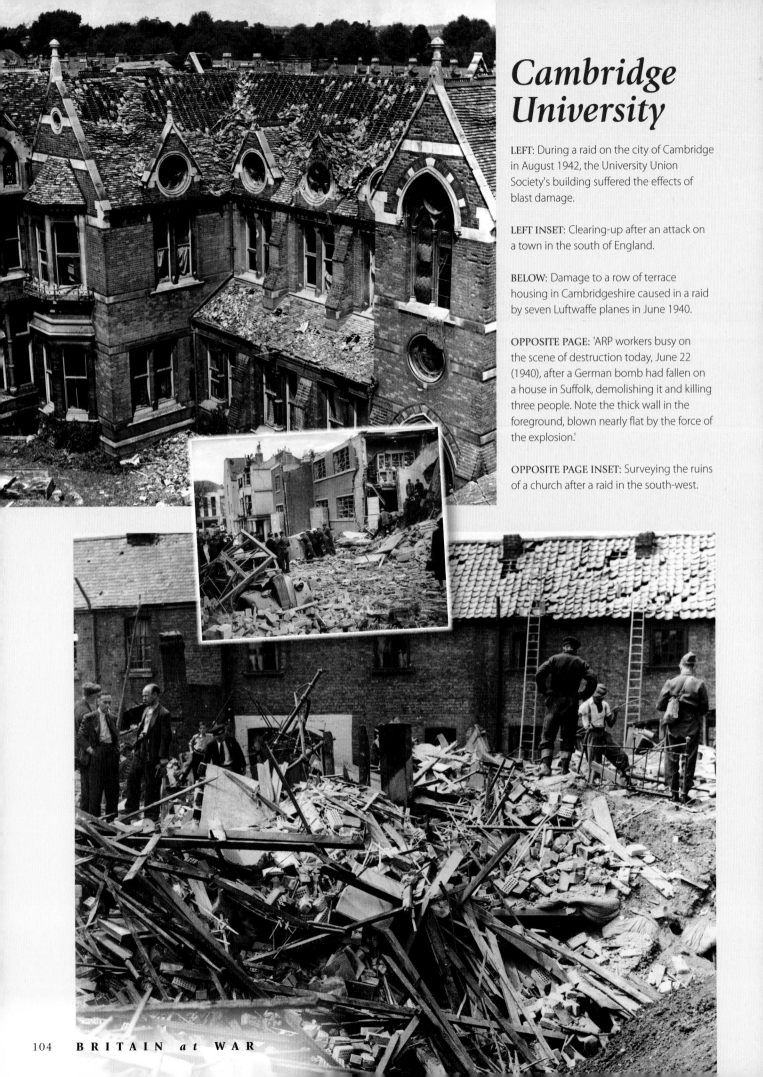

Cambridge University

LEFT: During a raid on the city of Cambridge in August 1942, the University Union Society's building suffered the effects of blast damage.

LEFT INSET: Clearing-up after an attack on a town in the south of England.

BELOW: Damage to a row of terrace housing in Cambridgeshire caused in a raid by seven Luftwaffe planes in June 1940.

OPPOSITE PAGE: 'ARP workers busy on the scene of destruction today, June 22 (1940), after a German bomb had fallen on a house in Suffolk, demolishing it and killing three people. Note the thick wall in the foreground, blown nearly flat by the force of the explosion.'

OPPOSITE PAGE INSET: Surveying the ruins of a church after a raid in the south-west.

Canterbury
Cathedral

RIGHT: As a city close to the south coast, and on a bomber path from the continent, Canterbury suffered a number of air attacks, the most severe of which took place on 1st June 1942 as part of the Baedeker raids. The family pictured here, salvaging among the ruins of their home, were saved by their Anderson shelter.

BELOW: The Archbishop of Canterbury inspects damage to the Cathedral caused by the raid in June 1940.

ABOVE TOP: Firemen hosing down the smouldering embers of a building in the centre of Canterbury.

ABOVE: Amazingly, no-one was hurt when a bomb damaged this house in West Common Road, Hayes, Kent.

LEFT: '"Military objective". This is the Kent Hospital in which women patients were killed during the night raid. This picture shows you one of the two smashed wards. Among the debris Sister Gantry crawled, giving morphia injections to the injured women while rescue work went on.'

Exeter first Baedeker target

LEFT: The cathedral town of Exeter was the first to be targeted in the series known as the Baedeker raids. On 24th April 1942, following the first attack, a pilot in a German broadcast is alleged to have said, 'We will go out and bomb every building in Britain marked with three stars in the Baedeker Guide'. Here women and children walk through damaged Exeter streets.

RIGHT ABOVE: A bomb crater in the foreground shows how close the four people sheltering safely in the Anderson shelter (middle ground) came to being killed in this raid in the eastern counties.

RIGHT MIDDLE: 'Two women pick their way through debris in a badly battered street in Exeter.'

BELOW: Exeter's mediaeval cathedral rises above the surrounding damaged streets; apart from broken windows it escaped unscathed.

OPPOSITE PAGE: The bombed ruins of St Michael's Church in Great Yarmouth. The seaside town on the Norfolk coast was attacked frequently, especially in 1941 when it was raided on 167 occasions, destroying much of the ancient town.

Brief raid on Bristol

BELOW: Rescue workers carry away an injured man from the wreckage of a Bristol building bombed during daylight hours in a brief hit-and-run attack on 28th August 1942.

LEFT: An ARP warden stands amidst the wreckage of a church in the Birmingham area after a night raid.

OPPOSITE ABOVE: Damage from the daylight attack on Bristol in August 1942. As a major port and site of the Bristol aircraft factory, the town was subjected to some of the most severe attacks of the war, with the city centre almost completely destroyed.

OPPOSITE PAGE BELOW RIGHT: 'Firemen and rescue squads at work among the debris of houses wrecked by Nazi bombs during the large scale attack on a Midlands' town last night.'

OPPOSITE PAGE BELOW LEFT: Damping down the fires in the remains of a bombed-out church, somewhere in the south-east.

Destroying homes

ABOVE AND OPPOSITE PAGE ABOVE: Workers comb through the wreckage of these homes to salvage the homeowners belongings, but also to reclaim building materials.

ABOVE INSET: Homes in Dover damaged by shells from German long-range guns.

LEFT: An air raid in Cambridgeshire killed nine people and destroyed eight homes.

BELOW: This Dornier which had machine-gunned streets in a coastal town was brought down on a beach at the beginning of September 1940.

OPPOSITE PAGE INSET: Mrs Chapman, aged 74, of the Home Counties, escaped injury after she decided to leave her bed and head for the shelter. She had just made it to the shelter when the bomb dropped.

OPPOSITE PAGE BELOW RIGHT: These once elegant homes close to the Dover seafront lie damaged and abandoned.

Dover shelled from the French coast

OPPOSITE PAGE ABOVE: On the south coast, and close to contintental Europe, Dover was an easy target for both air raids and long-range shelling. An air raid on 23rd March 1942 caused extensive damage. A number of people were trapped in the shelter beneath this building.

OPPOSITE PAGE INSET: This home in southern England was damaged in the first wave of flying bombs, nicknamed 'doodlebugs' or 'buzz bombs', in June 1944, exactly a week after the D Day landings.

OPPOSITE PAGE BELOW LEFT: A Dover sea-front hotel damaged by shelling. The censor did not pass this picture for publication.

OPPOSITE PAGE BELOW RIGHT: From the time France fell in May 1940, it became possible for German long-range guns, stationed on the northern French coast to reach the port of Dover. Over the course of the war, the town was shelled frequently. Here, a photographer captures the moment a shell bursts in a Dover street.

ABOVE: 'The coast of S. E. England as seen by the Germans across the Channel.'

LEFT: Two German planes attack a barrage balloon over Dover.

BELOW: Shells bursting on the Dover coast.

Bombed bus depot

OPPOSITE PAGE ABOVE AND BELOW: Following an air raid on Dover on 23rd March 1942 that left 13 people dead, a demolition squad works to clear the damage and debris in this bus garage.

OPPOSITE PAGE INSET: Damage to housing in Dover during the March 1942 raid.

RIGHT: School boys sorting through the wreckage of their school after the devastating raid on Coventry on 14th November 1940.

BELOW: The spire of St Michael's Church rises above the ruined streets of Coventry a month after the raid.

Petrol station set ablaze

OPPOSITE PAGE ABOVE: This petrol station was set ablaze when a bomb dropped during the Battle of Britain.

OPPOSITE PAGE BELOW: A shop and the home above wrecked as a result of a bomb blast 'somewhere in the south of England'.

LEFT: 'A boy with his cage of budgerigars beside the Anderson shelter in which they found safety while their home was wrecked by a bomb.' (18th July 1940)

BELOW: This house in the vicinity of the Thames Estuary was wrecked by a direct hit from a bomb.

Luftwaffe airmen captured

LEFT: Escorted by police, these Luftwaffe aircrew, shot down in the early weeks of the Blitz, are being transported to a PoW camp via a London station.

BELOW: This picture of two iron-crossed German airmen is ironically captioned: 'More Luftwaffe visitors here.'

OPPOSITE PAGE ABOVE: Hiding his face from the camera, this German airman is part of a large group being transported by rail through London in October 1940.

OPPOSITE PAGE BELOW: 'Their bombing days are over. Two Nazi airmen, who were brought down in a spot of action on the south coast, which is rapidly becoming known as the "graveyard of Nazi air-planes", entrain for their journey to prison camp.' (31st August 1940)

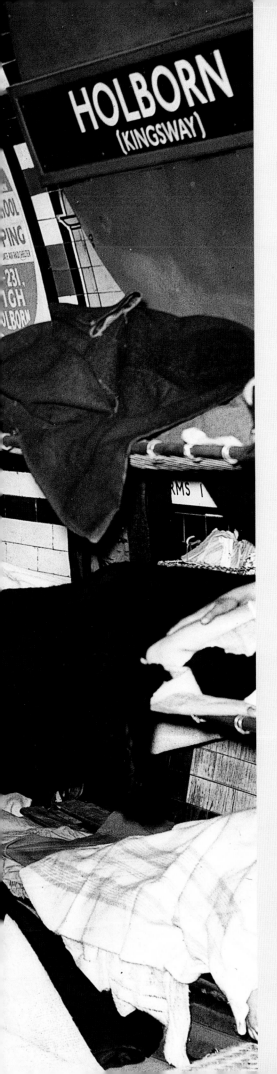

CHAPTER THREE

Defending the Home Front

Experience from the First World War and the Spanish Civil War alerted the government to the likelihood that aerial attack would make the British Isles a war front and that, even without an invasion, the risk of civilian deaths was great. Thus, from the early months of 1939 plans for civil defence were progressed. Air-raid shelters were delivered to thousands of homes and plans drawn up to evacuate children and other vulnerable people from areas thought to be at risk of bombing. Twelve regional Civil Defence Commissioners were appointed, with special powers to govern their areas should they become cut off from central government.

Resisting invasion

OPPOSITE PAGE: 'You are looking at the famous clock tower and the Houses of Parliament through a nearby barbed-wire entanglement – a symbolic picture that speaks of Britain's preparedness to withstand to the last any attempts at invasion.'

RIGHT: As part of a nationwide scheme to confuse any invaders landing in Britain by parachute, this village post office name sign is being painted over.

BELOW: Shortly after the retreat from Dunkirk, when invasion was a real possibility, there was an impetus to make Britain anonymous to invading troops. Painting out the name of this local railway stationaided that anonymity.

Sandbag duty

ABOVE: Residents filling sandbags to protect their homes on the day war was declared.

RIGHT: In order to prevent invading troops landing by plane, open areas that might present a landing site were covered with obstructions like these concrete tunnels.

OPPOSITE PAGE TOP: A scene in Hampstead in the first week of the war.

OPPOSITE PAGE BELOW RIGHT: Air Raid Protection (ARP) plans were already in place before the war started and both men and wome were recruited as ARP wardens whose job it was to ensure that the ARP regulations were adhered to and people kept safe.

OPPOSITE PAGE BELOW LEFT: 'Women residents of the Royal Borough of Kensington helping with the important job of sandbag filling.'

Protecting buildings

LEFT: Workmen filling sandbags to protect Southwark Town Hall. Sandbags helped to mitigate against the damage caused by shock waves from a bomb blast.

LEFT MIDDLE: The owner of this restaurant was taking no chances. Shopfronts with their large expanses of glass were particularly vulnerable to damage. Covering shopfronts in a trellis work of sticky paper was a more common method employed to minimise the chance of flying glass.

BELOW: 'A busy sandbagging scene in the West End of London.'

OPPOSITE PAGE: 'Reporting for duty – this scout cycled around the district delivering messages between ARP posts.'

OPPOSITE PAGE INSET: Even the humblest of builings needed protection!

IF YOU CARRY YOUR MASK YOU ARE AN ASSET IF NOT YOU ARE A LIABILITY TO ALL A.R.P. SERVICES

IMPORTANT

NOTICE OF AN **AIR RAID WARNING** BEING GIVEN WILL BE CONVEYED IMMEDIATELY TO THE AUDIENCE BY AN ANNOUNCEMENT FROM THE STAGE

Gas masks

Following the use of poison gas attacks on troops during the First World War, there was a real fear that Luftwaffe planes would drop not only explosive and incendiary devices but also poison gas bombs on civilian targets. In the months preceding the outbreak of war 38 million gas masks were distributed. There were Mickey Mouse-faced ones for young children and complete respirator suits for babies. Under ARP regulations it was an offence not to carry a gas mask at all times. However, as the war wore on no such attack transpired and the only times the public ever wore them were in practice drills and mock attacks. Soon these ugly and uncomfortable contraptions were forgotten items.

OPPOSITE PAGE TOP LEFT: ARP wardens were responsible for ensuring strict adherence to the various ARP regulations, including those relating to the carrying of gas masks.

OPPOSITE PAGE TOP RIGHT: When war was declared all places of entertainment were closed down in case of bombing. However, after a few weeks many had reopened with air-raid precautions in place. This sign is being carried into position as information for theatregoers.

OPPOSITE PAGE BELOW LEFT: This couple walk hand in hand down Regent Street in early October 1939; both carry their gas mask and steel helmet.

OPPOSITE PAGE BELOW RIGHT: Shortly after the outbreak of war, these young women walk through Hyde Park, each carrying her gas mask.

ABOVE: Shoppers in Southend prepared for a mock gas attack. Although there were frequent such mock attacks, the Germans never used poison gas in any of their raids.

BELOW: An everyday exchange with the milkman! In this 'mock' attack in Brighton tear gas was released.

Mock gas attack

OPPOSITE PAGE TOP LEFT: This huge box strapped to the handles of the pram carries the respirator suit that substituted for the adult gas mask.

OPPOSITE PAGE TOP RIGHT: These two young women carry customised gas-mask cases.

OPPOSITE PAGE BELOW: Chelsea pensioners, veterans from the previous century's wars, turn out with their gas masks.

ABOVE: George Street, Richmond, in May 1942 during a gas practice.

MIDDLE: A policeman directing pedestrians and traffic during the Richmond gas practice.

LEFT: The scene in Richmond in June 1942. Unlike the previous month, no one is carrying a gas mask. By this stage of the war gas masks were only carried during drills and practices.

Shelters

ARP wardens were responsible for the public shelters in their area, where those without their own shelter, or people caught away from home when the air-raid siren sounded, could take cover. However, many people had shelters in their own home or garden. The staple home shelter was the Anderson Shelter; four square metres in size, this was sunk into the garden and covered with half a metre of soil. Other shelters, like the Morrison shelter, were designed for construction within the home; some people preferred to shelter in cellars, basements and stairwells.

Large public shelters sometimes had heating, lighting and toilets, and a few had canteens. Getting a good night's sleep was always a problem – private shelters were stuffy and lacked basic facilities, but public shelters were noisy and full of restless people. The tunnels of the London Underground became a popular shelter for many Londoners during the Blitz, despite initial government attempts to discourage their use.

OPPOSITE PAGE TOP: A notice posted in Littlewood's store, Manchester, in the first weeks of the war.

MAIN PICTURE: 'Mr Frank Pinkerton of West Wickham has solved the problem of air raid sheltering in comfort. To his own design he has erected an air raid shelter in the lounge of his own home. The shelter which has room for six persons is built of thick concrete block, a curved roof giving great strength in case of house collapse. Fitted with bunks, carpets etc the family are enabled to sleep in security and comfort.'

LEFT: A small public shelter near Saunderton Station in High Wycombe, this had an internal diameter of 12 feet and a height of 6 feet.

BELOW: Adapted from the Borough tube, this was the largest air-raid shelter in Britain. It was able to hold 11,000 people and had eight entrances.

Safety and comfort

ABOVE: A London policeman designed and made these bunks for fitting into an Anderson Shelter; the Ministry for Home Security adopted the idea.

LEFT: An indoor 'table' shelter.

OPPOSITE PAGE: Athough early in the London Blitz the government, fearful that a 'deep shelter mentality' might develop, tried to discourage people from seeking shelter in London's tube stations. Public pressure, and the obvious evidence that this was not happening, made it relent.

Bedding down in the tube

MAIN PICTURE: At the beginning of the Blitz in September 1941, Londoners sleep on the escalators in a tube station. Facilities were not yet set up to cater for those sheltering in the London Underground.

OPPOSITE PAGE INSET: 'The warden sees that the children are "comfy" in their hammocks at the Aldwych underground railway, now opened to the public as an official refuge.'

BELOW TOP AND BOTTOM: By January 1941, bunks had been installed on Underground platforms and passengers waited for the last train while others settled down to sleep. The deep tunnels of the Underground offered a safe haven, but even they were not entirely bombproof. In one of the worst incidents of the war 110 people were killed while sheltering in, or travelling through, Bank tube station when it received a direct hit.

Shelter etiquette

ABOVE: A warden stands at the entrance to a public shelter in London.

ABOVE INSET: 'Two conflicting notices posted outside the well-sandbagged premises of a firm in the Strand are attracting the attention of passers-by. The first, put up in the name of the City of Westminster, intimates that a public air-raid shelter for 150 persons is inside the building. The other notice gives the opposite view of the firm.'

RIGHT: A notice asking able-bodied men not to shelter in the Underground.

Domestic shelters

LEFT: Although in an area subject to heavy bombardment and standing only 25 yards from where a bomb landed, this air-raid shelter, built from reinforced concrete, was undamaged. However, everyone knew that a shelter would not stand a direct hit.

BELOW: Some householders used their cellars as bomb shelters and it was necessary to ensure a emergency exit from the cellar in case the house above collapsed.

Protecting man's best friend

OPPOSITE PAGE TOP: Workers with the People's Dispensary for Sick Animals remove an injured dog from a bombed buliding.

OPPOSITE PAGE BELOW LEFT: Two men read a regional bulletin, produced by the Ministry of Information, posted in a London suburb.

OPPOSITE PAGE BELOW RIGHT: A message on the front door of this house lets others know that the homeowners are happy to share their shelter with other dog lovers and their pets.

LEFT: An injured dog is treated at one of the National ARP centres for animals.

BELOW: Demonstrating a series of aids to help people to be seen more clearly during the blackout.

The blackout

In order to make it as difficult as possible for enemy aircraft to sight their targets blackout regulations were brought into force. All buildings were required to conform and in the early weeks of enforcement blackout materials sold out rapidly. Windows had to be covered so that no chink of light escaped; vehicle lights had to be dimmed and only project downwards; streetlamps were fitted with a special screen which dimmed their light.

The one thing cited most consistently as most inconvenient about the war was the blackout, and as patrolling the blackout was one of the major tasks of Air Raid Protection (ARP) wardens, they were often seen as 'nagging' about maintaining those regulations. However, their job was vital to the safety and security of the neighbourhood they covered. Wardens had to deal with the immediate aftermath of a bomb falling in their area, inform central control and organise ambulance, fire and rescue services. They would also be expected to administer first aid and to ensure that people remained calm at any incident.

LEFT: An ARP outpost in Essex where the blackout shade and desk lamps throw shadows into the room.

INSET LEFT: Demonstrating a mask for a car headlamp to dim and divert the light downwards.

INSET RIGHT: Shop window displays also need to reduce illumination.

ABOVE: A candlelight service at Christ Church, West Green, Tottenham, in response to the blackout regulations.

INSET RIGHT: Sometimes the blackout was carried to extremes. This is a 'pipe-smoker's shield – at each pull the glow from the pipe is reflected forward.'

RIGHT: A policeman demonstrates a red-light torch used to pull up any speeding motorist caught exceeding the newly established 20 mph limit in built-up areas – a measure introduced to ensure pedestrian safety when streetlights were dimmed during the blackout.

The dimout

OPPOSITE PAGE ABOVE: By 17th September 1944, following the D-Day landings and the push through Europe, the war was going so well for the Allies that the threat of assault by Luftwaffe aircraft was deemed over. Blackout regulations were lifted, to be replaced by the 'dimout', which allowed an increase in luminosity. A street in Paddington pictured in the 'dimout'.

OPPOSITE PAGE BELOW: 'Tottenham Court Road looked almost pre-war last night when the new "maximum" lighting was switched on.'

ABOVE: Blackpool illuminations dimout-style.

RIGHT: Manchester was the first city to change to the brighter lighting.

Police work

The police force had many additional duties during the war. Burglary and other peacetime offences were much reduced but there were other crimes to tackle, such as black-market dealing and the theft that was often associated with it. One area that developed significantly was the imperative to monitor those suspected of sympathising with, or actively promoting, the Nazi way of life; there was also a need to investigate suspected German spies. The police took on innumerable other roles, from escorting prisoners of war to ensuring the public remained calm in the aftermath of an air raid.

LEFT TOP: In July 1940, th British Union of Fascists became subject to an official ban. In May of the same year their headquarters in Westminster had been raided; here a Scotland Yard detective escorts a woman, whose 'lightning' badge signals her fascist allegiance, from the building.

LEFT MIDDLE: Police take away documents and files during the raid on the British Union of Fascists headquarters.

LEFT BELOW: Crowds watch as the fascists are taken away by the police.

OPPOSITE PAGE TOP: There were Nazi sympathisers in all ranks of society. Here an armed guard waits at Folkestone Harbour for the return from Germany of Unity Mitford, daughter of Baron Redesdale and a devoted admirer of Hitler; she became known as the 'Storm Troop Maiden'.

BELOW LEFT: A policeman checks identity papers in a West End bar.

BELOW RIGHT: In April 1944, as the Allies prepared for the invasion of Europe, visitors were banned from going within 10 miles of the coast from the Wash to Land's End, and there was tight police control of that ban. Here, police check the papers of travellers at a south coast railway station.

PLEASE
HAVE
IDENTITY
CARDS
READY FOR
INSPECTION

Black marketeers

ABOVE: A wrist watch is valued on a street corner. The police fought a constant battle with black marketeers. Many of those involved in the black market had been involved in criminality before the war.

MIDDLE: This photographs shows money changing hands in a black-market deal in December 1945. Even after the end of the war shop prices and the quantities available for purchase were strictly controlled. Shopkeepers would keep unrationed goods 'under the counter' to be sold at the controlled price to regular customers; this was not an illegal practice as no-one profiteered. On the other hand, black marketeers obtained their goods in questionable, and frequently illegal, ways and sold them to the highest bidder.

RIGHT: Two American soldiers are approached by black marketeers at Rainbow Corner, Shaftesbury Avenue.

Protecting the home front

ABOVE: Oldham Police War Reserves receiving rifle instruction. Although the police remained unarmed on normal duty, there was a necessity for the force to be ready to defend the home front in the event of an invasion.

RIGHT: An air sentry receives the message 'enemy planes approaching'.

BELOW: 'Bren gunners in action against low-flying enemy aircraft.'

The big guns

OPPOSITE PAGE TOP: Anti-aircraft batteries were stationed all over the country with the aim of bringing down enemy bombers before they could drop their payload. Here, at an anti-aircraft unit somewhere in the north, the large anti-aircraft gun is brought into action.

OPPOSITE PAGE BELOW LEFT: Machine guns were capable of bringing down low-flying Luftwaffe planes, especially fighter aircraft.

OPPOSITE PAGE BELOW RIGHT: A gunner takes aim at a low-flying enemy aircraft.

ABOVE: Using the height-finding apparatus which helped target the large anti-airctaft guns.

RIGHT: Loading the gun with anti-aircraft shells.

The Observer Corps

RIGHT: Two members of the Observer Corps on duty at sundown. Anti-aircraft units relied on the Observer Corps to signal the approach of enemy aircraft. Staffed by civilians, the corps was operationally controlled by Fighter Command. Full-time members worked 48 hours per week but many were part-time, working shifts in addition to other jobs.

MIDDLE INSET: A gunner carries anti-aircraft shells, ready for loading into the gun.

BELOW: 'An observer identifies a plane while his colleague plots the course.'

BOTTOM: Dawn breaks on an Observer Corps listening post.

Women in the corps

LEFT: Mrs Schofield and Mrs Fenwick, members of the Observer Corps, study books on aircraft recognition.

BELOW: 'Mrs Schofield is relieved at her post by her husband, also a Corps member, despite a full-time job as a draughtsman.'

First Aid

RIGHT: These volunteers at the London Homeopathic Hospital took part in research to monitor the effects of, and develop possible remedies for, mustard gas poisoning in the event of a German gas attack.

BELOW: Members of the public, attending a lecture on First Aid at the Westminster Hospital in June 1940, watch as a doctor and an ARP warden demonstrate how to apply a tourniquet. The event was so popular that hundreds of people had to be turned away.

Roof spotters

LEFT: The quickest way of informing factories and institutions of approaching enemy aircraft was by deploying teams of roof spotters, who had the additional duty of spotting fires that might break out as a result of incendiary devices. Here a pair of roof spotters carry out their duties on the top of the *Daily Mail* building, with St Paul's in the background.

RIGHT TOP: Roof spotters receiving training in aircraft recognition from an RAF officer.

RIGHT BELOW: 'An RAF officer pointing out a British type of plane overhead.'

Fit defenders

OPPOSITE PAGE: These men are leading a recruiting drive, just after the retreat from Dunkirk in June 1940; its aim was to encourage men to get themselves fit to join the military or home defence units.

RIGHT: As part of their training at the Empire Stadium, Wembley, these men are using ash sticks, which weighed approximately the same as service rifles.

INSET: Volunteer recruits of all ages gathered at Bradford Park Avenue Football Ground on Saturday, 22nd June 1940, to take part in the 'Fitness For Service' drills organised by the Central Council of Recreative Physical Training.

BELOW: Resistance training!

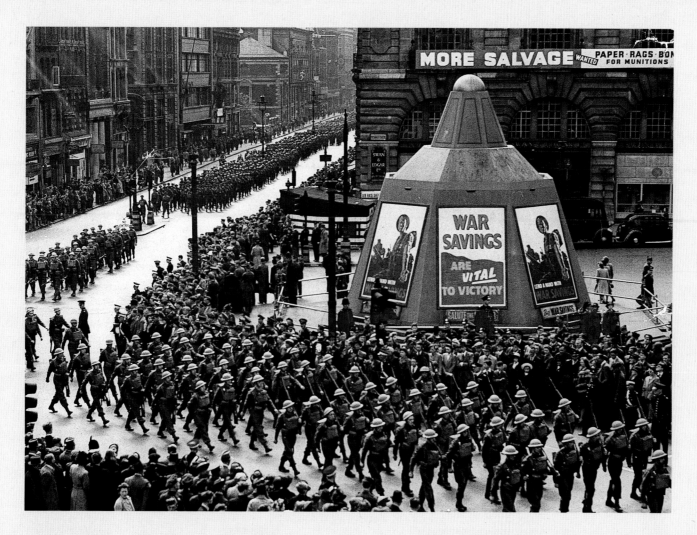

Dad's Army

The Home Guard, or Dad's Army as it was affectionately known, is one of the most iconic ideas of Britian's civil defence strategy. Originally called Local Defence Volunteers (LDV), it was set up as the Blitzkrieg overran Europe and the British Expeditionary Force was pushed back to the beaches at Dunkirk. By July of 1940, the newly installed prime minister, Winston Churchill, had changed the name from the LDV to the Home Guard.

At first there were no uniforms; Home Guard members were identified by armbands. The units had no modern weapons, only old shotguns, pitchforks and sticks. Although many of the volunteers were old men, many had combat experience, having served in the First World War. Over the next four years, until it was disbanded in November 1944, the Home Guard

developed until it was almost indistinguishable in its professionalism from the regular army. Well kitted out in uniforms and weaponry, it was a well drilled force, capable of taking on many of the duties the regular army had previously undertaken.

OPPOSITE PAGE: A Home Guard unit on parade. Many of the members of the Home guard were old men, veterans of the Great War, and their earlier training and combat experience was a valuable resource.

OPPOSITE PAGE INSET LEFT: These men parading in June 1940 wear LDV armbands. As the German Blitzkrieg advanced through France, a call went out to all men 'not presently engaged in military service between the ages of 17 and 65' to volunteer to help fight off an invasion. In the first week quarter of a million volunteered; some women also joined up.

OPPOSITE PAGE INSET RIGHT: Major General Cecil Pereira takes the salute from early LDV units as they march through London.

ABOVE: Men of the Home Guard parade in Piccadilly Circus in May 1944. They are indistinguishable from regular military.

Home Guard expertise

LEFT: A queue of men forms to join the Parachute Defence Corps at Loughton in Essex. As the Home Guard took over duties normally undertaken by regular soldiers, there was a need for such specialist units.

BELOW: In August 1940, with the real prospect of a German invasion, these men manufacture 'Molotov cocktails' for the Home Guard to use against German armoured divisions.

OPPOSITE PAGE TOP: The *Daily Mail*'s Home Guard unit on parade.

OPPOSITE PAGE BELOW: The company unit is inspected by Viscount Rothermere, owner of the *Daily Mail*.

Defending Parliament...

LEFT: Lord Strabolgi, a member of the Parliamentary Home Guard unit stationed in Westminster Hall and staffed by members of both Houses as well as parliamentary officials and reporters, stands on duty in the snow of Palace Yard.

ABOVE TOP: A Home Guard unit marches in to take over guard duties at Buckingham Palace. As the war progressed and the Home Guard became more professional, it took over guarding key sites.

ABOVE BELOW: King George inspects Home Guard units at a rally at Worcester Park.

...and Buckingham Palace

ABOVE: The 1st County London (Westminster) Battalion take on guard duties at Buckingham Palace in May 1941.

RIGHT INSET: Certificate issued to the 1,701,208 men and 31,824 women who had served their country in the Home Guard.

BELOW RIGHT: Home Guard units march in their final parade before being disbanded in November 1944.

BELOW LEFT: Posting sentries at Buckingham Palace as the Home Guard take on duties.

In the years when our Country
was in mortal danger

THOMAS ATKINS

who served 4 July 1940 – 31 December 1944

gave generously of his time and powers to make himself ready for her defence by force of arms and with his life if need be.

George R.I.

THE HOME GUARD

Fighting fires

ABOVE: One hundred hoses at full blast in a demonstration by Wolverhampton Auxiliary Fire Service.

LEFT: London's firefighters faced their greatest challenge during, and after, the raid on 29th December 1940 when a Luftwaffe raid set thousands of fires across the city. Here firefighters try to prevent the spread of the fire beneath St Paul's Cathedral.

OPPOSITE PAGE TOP: The morning after the raid, fire crews, after fighting the blaze all night, start to clear up their equipment.

OPPOSITE PAGE BELOW: As daylight arrives on 30th December, firefighters in some areas continue the struggle for control.

Keeping the public safe

As most people slept quietly in their beds at night or kept safe in shelters during an air raid, there were large numbers of people on duty throughout the night. ARP wardens were supported by other workers and volunteers such as police, medical and fire services. The dedication of firefighters saved many lives and a great deal of property. Incendiary bombs, which were designed to start fires, caused them most work but explosive bombs also caused fires, especially if they ruptured a gas main.

OPPOSITE PAGE TOP: Firefighters fill cans with petrol which will fuel the pumps to raise water pressure to the fire hoses.

OPPOSITE PAGE BELOW: Amidst the bomb ruins, a fireman damps down the embers of a fire set off in an air raid.

LEFT: A female fire-fighter waits for orders from a comrade fighting the flames from a balcony on a burning building.

BELOW: While colleagues remain at work damping down burnt-out buildings in Fore Street, this fireman clears away his equipment.

BOTTOM: Firemen play their hoses on a fire sparked by an incendiary device.

The aftermath of a raid

For civilians, air raids posed the greatest danger to life and limb; protecting the public from such danger was where the major civil defence efforts were required. In the immediate aftermath of a bomb dropping a range of people would be involved – ARP wardens, police, firefighters, rescue workers, doctors, nurses, ambulance staff. However, there were also tasks to be undertaken in the days and months following; people affected often needed care, both physically and emotionally, and demolition crews and others worked to remove rubble and debris to make the area safe.

RIGHT: Royal Engineers working among the ruined buildings of the City of London in the week following the Fire of London. Their job was to set off controlled explosions to bring down unsafe masonry.

BELOW: A welcome break and a cup of tea for these firemen.

OPPOSITE PAGE TOP: In the aftermath of a bomb landing many people and organisations were involved in rescue operations – ARP, the Heavy Rescue brigade, the police, and often the military and civilians also helped. In this rescue in Folkestone after a V2 attack in October 1944, American soldiers, Home Guard and British sailors are all involved.

OPPOSITE PAGE BELOW RIGHT: The Salvation Army offers tea to the firefighters. This was just one of several volunteer organisations that provided refreshments for those on duty or civilians caught in air raids.

OPPOSITE PAGE BELOW LEFT: Unsafe masonry tumbles as a result of explosive charges set by Royal Engineers.

Demolishing the danger

ABOVE: After London's first night raid in late August 1940, demolition squads work to make safe a damaged bank.

RIGHT: A demolition squad at work on a bombed house – one of the gang is working at the end of a rope making the roof safe. In the foreground another man works on a street lamp, many of which were still gas-powered at this time.

OPPOSITE PAGE TOP: Royal Engineers laying a gun cotton charge in preparation for a controlled explosion to demolish an unsafe wall.

OPPOSITE PAGE BELOW: A policeman cycles through a London street to signal the 'All Clear' after an air-raid drill in the first week of the war.

CHAPTER FOUR

Uniformed services

As soon as the war started there was a need for a large increase in the armed forces; consequently, the number of young men in uniform increased. However, these were not the only people to don uniforms during the war and serve the country, either voluntarily or through conscription. There were half a million women in the British forces, most of whom served within the British Isles. Apart from the military, there were a whole host of civilian groups who spent at least part of their time in uniform – ARP wardens, the Home Guard, Firefighters, the Observer Corps, the Voluntary Ambulance Service, the Women's Land Army, to name but a few. For them, their uniform provided practical and protective clothing suited to the particular functions they were required to undertake, while also helping to build a sense of unity and team spirit, making them identifiable to others within and outside the unit.

Conscription

The declaration of war resulted in the necessity for a supply of men to form a fighting force. They were recruited from several sources. There were already sizeable cohorts of Regulars or Territorials in all branches of the military. While many volunteered with the declaration, a Conscription Bill had been introduced in May 1939, and soon afterwards all young men under 21 were registered, ready to be called up when needed.

As the war progressed, the age for conscription widened to include men between 18 and 50, and also single women between the ages of 20 and 30. Most conscripted men were sent into the army, and by June 1941 two-and-a-quarter million were in the service.

OPPOSITE PAGE ABOVE: Members of the ground crew of 603 (City of Edinburgh) Fighter Squadron pose with their Alsatian mascot. The 'kills' that the pilot of the plane had made are recorded in the crosses painted on the side of the cockpit.

OPPOSITE PAGE BELOW LEFT: 'Jimmy London, aged a full four, has a chat about this war with a soldier he has met while waiting for an evacuation train.'

OPPOSITE PAGE BELOW RIGHT Sailors start their leave with a cigar, emulating Winston Churchill, who at this point in the war, October 1939, was serving as First Lord of the Admiralty.

ABOVE: Soldiers who helped run the service during a bus strike in London in 1944, collect their blankets at Hammersmith Garage before bedding down in the buses.

RIGHT: A soldier passing by Westminster Cathedral slips in to pray in March 1941.

Waiting for the call to fight

The evacuation from Dunkirk in June 1940 was a triumph in that it rescued the men, but most of the army's equipment was left behind. With the increasing numbers of conscripted men adding to the rescued soldiery, Britain had a large combat-ready force without the tools to retake 'fortress' Europe. Thus, for much of the next year there were millions of soldiers stationed all over Britain, waiting for the call to fight. For the munitions industry there was a huge job to be done replacing and increasing stocks of equipment and weaponry.

The soldiers stationed throughout the country proved a useful supply of manpower to help with harvests and many other projects, from fortifying the beaches to guarding sensitive installations. They also helped fight fires and repair bomb damage during and after air raids. As the war progressed, soldiers were seen out and about, becoming important members of the communites in which they were stationed.

ABOVE: 'Our troops are constantly carrying out exercises in which they practise dealing with a force of enemy which is assumed to have landed on the coast. In this way they keep themselves fit and accustomed to the techniques of seashore fighting.'

OPPOSITE PAGE ABOVE: Troopers from the London Irish Regiment at training with rifles and fixed bayonets. At this time, October 1940, despite the failure of Hitler's invasions plans for September, there remained the fear of an enemy landing.

OPPOSITE PAGE BELOW RIGHT: A member of the Royal Fusiliers at revolver practice on a South Coast beach in June 1941.

OPPOSITE PAGE BELOW LEFT: August 1940, post-Dunkirk and at the height of the Battle of Britain, Black Watch soldiers stationed on the South Coast are pictured during a training exercise to repel an attempt to land German paratroopers.

On home leave

ABOVE: This soldier is greeted by his family as he returns home on leave for ten days during April 1940.

RIGHT: The wedding of Private George Pinnock to Miss Joan Cox on 25th April 1940 at St Stephen's Church, Rochester Row, Victoria. The groom was on a 72-hour pass from his regiment, the Highland Light Infantry, and they were to see each other just once more in the next five years.

OPPOSITE PAGE: Two British soldiers, on leave from France, telephone home from the train station to announce that they have just got back to Britain.

OPPOSITE PAGE INSET: This soldier, greeted by two members of his family, was able to write home to let them know when he would be back on leave.

Invalided home

ABOVE: Invalided soldiers recuperate at Hatfield House, Hertfordshire, which was commandeered for the duration and turned into a military hospital.

LEFT: A member of the British Expeditionary Force is brought home wounded, following one of the first battles in the blitzkrieg of May 1940, which was to result in the retreat from Dunkirk.

OPPOSITE PAGE ABOVE LEFT: A soldier with leg wounds has his needs attended to by a nurse at a hospital in Southern England.

OPPOSITE PAGE ABOVE RIGHT: This soldier, wounded in the eyes, is being entertained using headphones attached to a wireless. He is being cared for at St Dunstan's Convalescent Home near Brighton, which was converted into a special hospital for those suffering from eye injuries.

OPPOSITE PAGE BELOW: Recuperating from injuries sustained at Dunkirk, soldiers enjoy a game of billiards with the nurses.

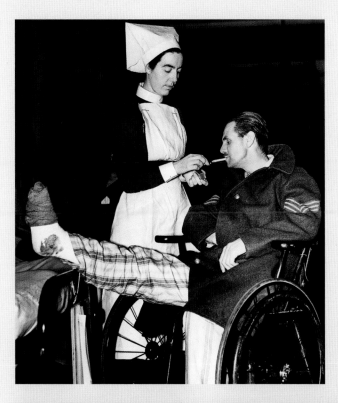

Service in the Navy

During the 'phoney war' the Navy was the service which endured the greatest loss of life. This was as a result of its duty to protect British merchant ships carrying essential supplies of food and raw materials across the Atlantic from the USA. Convoys of British ships were hunted, harried and attacked by German U-boats, often working together in teams nicknamed 'wolf packs'. At the beginning of the war the German navy had only 28 U-boats but their success in sinking supply ships encouraged the building of more.

When Stalin's Russia joined Britain against the Germans in June 1941, British convoys braved the freezing conditions of the north-west passage to supply the USSR. And for three years between 1940 and 1943 there was a need to keep the the island of Malta supplied while Italian and German naval forces sought superiority in the Mediterranean.

OPPOSITE PAGE ABOVE: *HMS Victory*, Nelson's old ship, was pressed into service as a training ship. Here two British sailors sit on the wooden deck, surrounded by old-style blocks and ropes, to write home.

OPPOSITE PAGE BELOW: Sailors from *HMS Ganges* off on Christmas leave in 1940.

RIGHT ABOVE: Survivors from the destroyer *Gurkha*, which was attacked in the North Sea by at least 30 Dorniers, board a bus to take them on leave.

RIGHT MIDDLE TOP: Looking cheerful and relieved, men from the aircraft carrier *Ark Royal*, torpedoed in the Mediterranean in November 1941, arrive back in England.

MIDDLE BELOW: 'This is the happiest picture you have seen for a long time and one which depicts the great paternal quality of our sailors. These two sailors in the cheeriest of moods, carry their babies for their wives while on their way to the station while returning from leave.'

BOTTOM: These men being fitted out with new kit are survivors from the aircraft carrier *Courageous*, sunk in September 1939 in the Atlantic. Five hundred men died when *Courageous* went down.

LEFT MIDDLE TOP: This sailor, a survivor from the sinking of the cruiser *Effingham* off Norway in June 1940, wears soldier's battledress but displays naval insignia on his cap, breast and arm.

RAF glamour

The men of the RAF had the most glamorous profile of all the services. Their uniforms were more attractive in cut and colour and the tasks they were asked to carry out generated connotations of danger, heroism and romance. In 1939 the RAF was only 21 years old, having been formed at the end of the First World War from the Royal Flying Corps when air warfare was in its infancy. Just as it was a young service, many of the men were also young. But there was no disguising the danger – from the approximately 600,000 men who served 150,000 were killed. It was the service which became the front line in the Battle of Britain, after the army's retreat from Dunkirk, and the service which scored the first notable victory against the enemy.

MAIN PICTURE: 'The crew of a bomber have a few moments rest on the tender of bombs which will shortly be loaded onto their machine, to be dropped on some specified objective in Germany'.

INSET ABOVE: Ground crew from the navy's Fleet Air Arm at work on a new Voigt-Sikorski 'Chesapeake' dive-bomber, nicknamed the 'cheesecake' by the men. The bomber, designed and made in the USA, was made available to Britain under the Lend-Lease Agreement, made in March 1941.

INSET BELOW: Pictured during the Battle of Britain, this crew had just returned from helping to repel a 100-plane-strong Luftwaffe attack.

Resting between sorties

OPPOSITE PAGE ABOVE: RAF pilots sleep and play games in their rest room at their base 'somewhere in Scotland'.

OPPOSITE PAGE BELOW: 'The men of the RAF Fighter Squadrons are ever on the alert, whether at work or during their brief hours of relaxation. This picture, taken at the County of London Squadron of the Fighter Command, shows the spirit which prevails amongst these men at all times and which has spurred them on to render their unforgettable service to their country.'

ABOVE: As they rest between sorties during one of the biggest battles of the Battle of Britain, squadron members listen to the account of a New Zealand flyer who had to bail out when he was shot down.

ABOVE: RAF cyclists carrying food to feed Barrage Balloon crews. Most of the Barrage Balloon sites were without catering facilities and so food was prepared at a central depot and then transported in hay boxes which kept everything piping hot, even over distances of 10 miles.

Leaping into action

MAIN PICTURE: Fighter pilots leap into action and rush to their planes after a warning from HQ that an unidentified plane had been spotted by the Observer Corps.

OPPOSITE PAGE INSET: During his tour of Fighter Stations in June 1940, the King met with members of a squadron about to leave for a flight over enemy territory.

BELOW: 'In the Operations Room of Air Defence Headquarters are the brains of the whole defence system. Here are the telephonists around the map on which they place and move models of raiders.'

BELOW INSET: RAF ground crews move a Heinkel to a secret air base where it can be researched to gain information about Luftwaffe aircraft.

Women's corps

Each of the three services, Army, Navy and Airforce, maintained female auxiliary corps. Although after the First World War the Women's Royal Naval Service (WRNS or Wrens) and the Women's Auxiliary Air Force (WAAF) had been disbanded, both corps were re-formed in April 1939. However, the Auxiliary Territorial Service (ATS) had remained between the wars as a reserve of trained women to assist the army in the event of war. There were also a number of smaller women's corps which undertook specific duties – for example the Voluntary Aid Detachment (VAD) nurses who served in military hospitals and the Air Transport Auxiliary Service whose female pilots delivered planes and essential supplies.

ABOVE: Canadian troops break for a cup of tea during an exercise to test London's defences. In the exercise, which took place in July 1941, these soldiers played the part of German invaders.

ABOVE INSET: In April 1940, VAD nurses greet and offer support to military families returning home to Britain from garrisons in the Far East.

RIGHT: A policeman wears his wartime uniform; the protective tin helmet was the principal change to the pre-war uniform.

OPPOSITE PAGE ABOVE: Groups of uniformed civil defence workers on a march past during a Civil Defence Service in St Paul's; King George received the salute.

OPPOSITE PAGE MIDDLE: After VE Day, these British soldiers were being flown out by the RAF to the Far East to supplement the force fighting in the region.

OPPOSITE PAGE BELOW: Women recruits to 'NAAFI' (Navy, Army and Air Force Institutes) being drilled by an army sergeant at their base in Watford.

Allied troops

The military forces from many countries served the Allied cause, and several of them had units stationed in Britain. Thousands of French troops had been rescued from the beaches in June 1940 and they joined a growing band of military groups, such as the remnants of the Polish forces, who had managed to escape Hitler's blitzkrieg and had set up bases in Britain. Until January 1942, the largest contingents of foreign soldiers stationed in Britain came from the British colonies; after that date, growing numbers of American soldiers, or GIs, added to the number of military uniforms seen on the streets of Britain.

OPPOSITE PAGE ABOVE: The first contingent of American soldiers land in Northern Ireland after being shipped across the Atlantic.

OPPOSITE PAGE BELOW: Irish women and children greet the American Expeditionary Force as it lands in Britain to set up camp in Ulster under the command of Major General Russell P. Hartle.

BELOW AND RIGHT: The first GIs in Northern Ireland take refreshments on landing. It was just seven weeks after the Japanese raid on Pearl Harbor on 7th December 1941, which drew the USA into the war.

BOTTOM: As they march through the streets of Northern Ireland, American soldiers, nicknamed 'Doughboys', make friends with the local populace. It was the start of what was to be a complex relationship between the British people and the American soldiers.

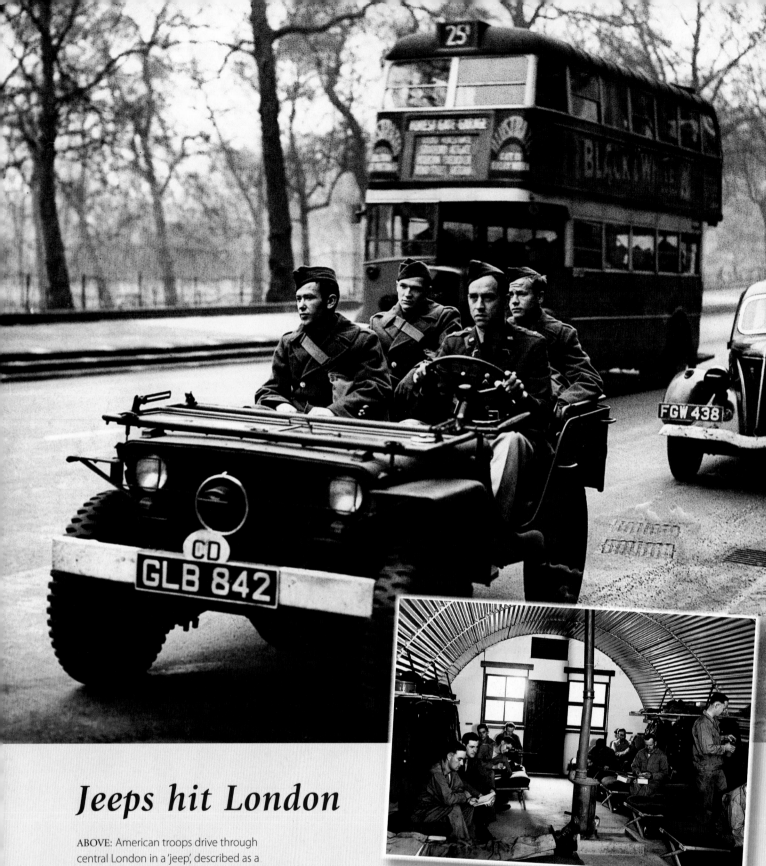

Jeeps hit London

ABOVE: American troops drive through central London in a 'jeep', described as a 'baby reconnaissance car'.

RIGHT: GIs stationed in a rapidly erected hut, on a USA Army camp in the Home Counties, built to house the growing numbers of American troops stationed in Britain.

OPPOSITE PAGE MAIN PICTURE: 'A race for the canteen. These doughboys will be racing with even greater zest for the "second front" one day.'

OPPOSITE PAGE INSET: American troops arrived in London in early March 1942 and a group are pictured here in Traflagar Square.

Mixing with the locals

ABOVE: American troops help out by constructing emergency housing for Londoners bombed out of their homes.

RIGHT MIDDLE: Brian Lee, aged 9, gets a helping hand from an American soldier, who straightens his tie before he leaves for the country in an evacuee party.

RIGHT BELOW The US flag hangs at half mast in Shaftesbury Avenue on 13th April 1945 as a mark of respect for President Roosevelt who had died unexpectedly the day before, less than four weeks before the surrender of Germany and VE Day.

OPPOSITE PAGE: American military relax as the landlord of the village pub serves beer.

Making friends

ABOVE: Two women in Trafalgar Square are snapped by an American soldier.

RIGHT MIDDLE: This American soldier cycled to Ascot and worked alongside a local to pick the winners.

RIGHT BELOW: Joan Clarke, of the National Fire Service, offers a light to a newly arrived American soldier, Sergeant Frank Dardanell from Verona, Pennsylvania.

OPPOSITE PAGE: Armed with a carbine, a US soldier stops a bus in a London street in May 1944 [ABOVE]. On the bus the identity papers of all military personnel are examined [BELOW LEFT]. 'American soldiers whose papers did not satisfy civil and military police were taken away in Army lorries.' [BELOW RIGHT] In the run up to D Day, it was important that all military personnel were engaged on training and preparation for the landings.

GIs on parade

LEFT: March 1943 and ranks of American troops march along the Embankment from Westminster to Trafalgar Square, as part of the Allied Wings for Victory Parade.

OPPOSITE PAGE ABOVE: 'For the first time since 1917, US troops paraded through London when they marched from Grosvenor Square to the City of London to lunch at the Guildhall with the Lord Mayor. Headed by a band, three hundred US troops and twenty marines in full ceremonial dress were cheered by London crowds along the entire route of their march.' (3rd September 1942)

OPPOSITE PAGE BELOW: The 14th Major Port Transportation Corps of the US Army march through the ancient Bargate of Southampton with fixed bayonets and colours flying in March 1946. They were the first foreign troops to be granted this privilege because of their close association with the port during the war. Over 2,000,000 US troops embarked at Southampton.

United Nations Day

ABOVE: The Kings of (l – r) Norway, Yugoslavia and Britain, take the salute on United Nations Day on 14th June 1942. The formation of the United Nations did not come until April 1945.

RIGHT MIDDLE: The view from Buckingham Palace of the United Nations Day Parade.

RIGHT BELOW: Allied Forces parade through Trafalgar Square on United Nations Day.

Demobilisation

Throughout 1944, 1945 and 1946 there was a gradual demobilisation of all the uniformed corps. The Home Guard was disbanded in November 1944, as the threat of an invasion disappeared. After the Victory in Europe in May 1945, a million men and women were demobilised from the armed forces, and many of the other civilian volunteer forces such as the ARP Service were stood down permanently. After VJ day military demobilisation continued, but it was a huge undertaking. There had been over five million people in armed service at the peak of wartime need, and it took until 1947 for all of them to be demobbed. With the standing down of the wartime military machine came the start of National Service, in effect, an extension of the conscription introduced in 1939, but in this case it only required young men of 18 to serve for two years.

RIGHT ABOVE: Starting with a service in Westminster Abbey a week of Thanksgiving for the Victory began on 16th September 1945. The date coincided with the fifth anniversary of the Battle of Britain and here the great Battle of Britain fly-past is captured as squadrons in formation tear across the London skyline.

RIGHT MIDDLE: The pilots and crews of the RAF were given the honour of leading the Thanksgiving procession down the Mall to the Abbey.

RIGHT BELOW: Royal Marine Commandos parade through Trafalgar Square during Thanksgiving week.

Entertaining the troops

OPPOSITE PAGE: Singer, Paddy Prior entertains the troops of the British Expeditionary Force on Sunday 8th October 1939, a couple of days before they embarked for France.

OPPOSITE PAGE INSET: At the same concert for the BEF the troops add their own talents to the open air concert.

RIGHT ABOVE: 'The army of today's all right. First-class entertainment, and an all-star show at that. The ATS girls were mingling with anti-aircraft gunners – men from lonely stations over Britain – at Drury Lane yesterday (27th March 1940), watching a special performance arranged by NAAFI.'

RIGHT MIDDLE: 'Miss Paddy Prior, one of the ENSA entertainers, amongst the troops as she sings a popular song.'

BELOW RIGHT: A scene from the RAF's musical play *Seven boys leave with Cinderfella* at the Wintergarden Theatre.

BELOW LEFT: The audience applaud Jack Hylton's Band playing at the Royal Artillery Theatre in Woolwich.

Sporting performance

ABOVE: Station staff from Waterloo entertain the troops in the YMCA canteen.

RIGHT: A small section of the audience of 1500 Guards who enjoyed a performance of *Shepherd's Pie* in April 1940.

OPPOSITE PAGE ABOVE: 'A scene at Upton Park where West Ham United played Leicester City showing the usual football fans watching the game – in Army uniform'. This picture was taken the day before war was declared.

OPPOSITE PAGE MIDDLE: RAF men in France at New Year 1940 receive games equipment – footballs, quoits and boxing gloves – in order to occupy the waiting time during the 'phoney war'.

OPPOSITE PAGE BELOW: A special performance of *The Women* at Golders Green Hippodrome for the Queen's Westminsters. The regiment's Lance-Corporal, Peter Mather, was released from duty to stage-manage the production.

Entertaining the public

MAIN PICTURE AND INSET: The forces often put on entertainments for the public, frequently as part of savings drives to encourage people to invest their money in war bonds. Here the band of the Grenadier Guards performs in Trafalgar Square to a huge crowd.

BELOW: The Guards band playing on top of an air raid shelter in Trafalgar Square, while the youngster in the foreground plays in the empty fountain pool.

BELOW RIGHT: Dance halls became very popular. It was a place for young men and women to meet, make contact with one another, and listen to popular band music. When the American GIs arrived they brought with them new music and dances like the jitterbug.

OPPOSITE PAGE BELOW RIGHT: These instruments were left behind by the 3rd Division of the Royal Canadian Army Corps. In the background a soldier keeps the crowd at bay while the small boy surveys the scene.

OPPOSITE PAGE BELOW LEFT: Loading up cinema equipment to be used to entertain RAF crews stationed overseas during the 'phoney war'.

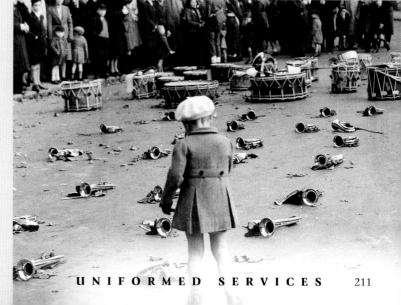

CHAPTER FIVE

Women at work

When the war started there was a necessity for labour on all fronts. Pre-war the workforce was largely male, but many of those men were required for the military. By 1940 Britain had three and a half million men in the armed forces. However, there was a need to keep essential services, like power and transport, running and a need to produce the munitions necessary to fight the war. The war itself created a large number of new jobs, from ARP wardens and fire spotters to demolition crews. Other jobs, like those in the fire service, required an increase in numbers to deal with the effects of war on civilian life. Women were the only pool of labour from which to recruit to breach the shortfall caused by the loss of so many male workers. To this end Winston Churchill, in January 1940, when First Lord of the Admiralty, called for a million women to help with war work, principally in the prouction of munitions.

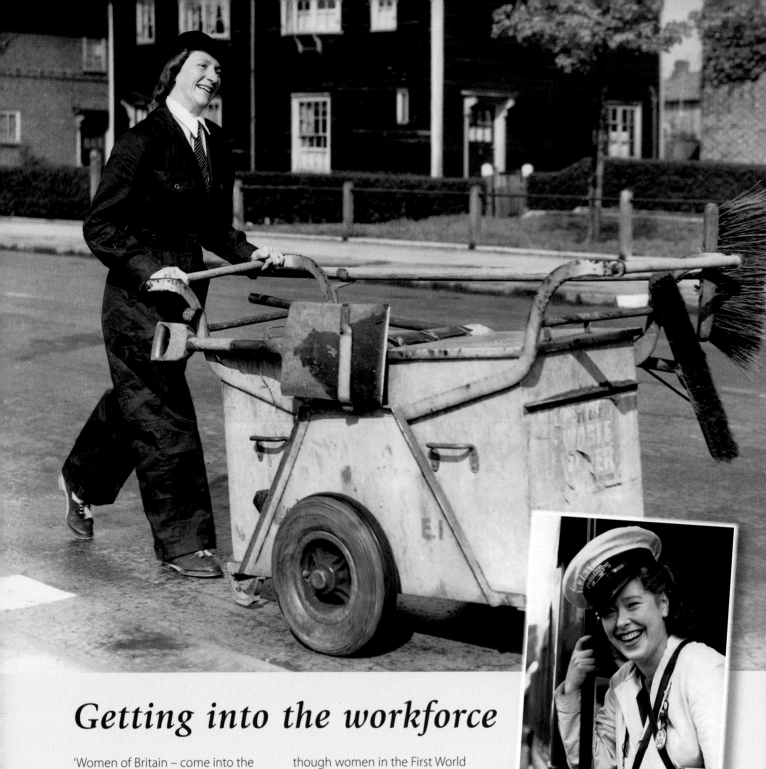

Getting into the workforce

'Women of Britain – come into the factories' is one of the most well known slogans from the propaganda posters of the war but the majority of women in pre-war Britain had never worked in a factory; indeed few women had paid employment. It would not be unusual for a woman to marry and move from the parental home to living with her husband never having had a paid job. Those who did work outside the home normally left as soon as they married; many employers would not hire married women. Even though women in the First World War had gone into the workforce to aid the country, social convention, reinforced by the depression of the thirties, re-established the idea that paid employment was for men, the 'breadwinners' in the family.

Women responded to the calls for them to 'come into the factories' as well as taking on numerous other jobs: driving buses, glazing bomb-damaged windows, mending roads, delivering the post. working as shop assistants, being part of a demolition team, to name but a few. The diverse range of jobs undertaken by women, while not contributing directly to the war effort, were essential in maintaining morale and keeping the country run smoothly.

OPPOSITE PAGE: Mrs C. Miles of Mill Hill was employed by Hendon Council as a street sweeper.

OPPOSITE PAGE INSET: Miss Birdie Mahoney trains as a bus conductress in Cambridge.

RIGHT: 'Miss Bambridge, of Coombe Hill, took a job as a butcher at Kingston-on-Thames.

BELOW RIGHT: Conductresses on the Brighton trolley bus service set a national record with an absentee rate of less than one per cent.

BELOW MIDDLE: 'A trousered girls cleaning the window of a London teashop. With many thousands of men now in the Services, a good many of their jobs have to be carried out by women.'

BELOW LEFT: A woman paints replicas of the goods sold inside on to the boards that cover the bomb-shattered windows of this ladies' clothes shop.

Conscription

When Winston Churchill called for a million women to help with war work, it was only one of many calls for women workers, and although many responded to these calls, the country could never quite fill the labour gap. In December 1941 women between the ages of 20 and 30, described as 'mobile' – that is, they had no pressing responsibilities in the home – were conscripted to do war work, either in the forces or in industry. The age for conscription was extended throughout 1942, so that by 1943 nine out of ten single women and eight out of ten married women with children over the age of fourteen were either in the forces or in 'essential work'. Even women classed as 'immobile' took on part-time jobs outside the home or became 'outworkers', a role that involved making or assembling small machine parts in the home.

OPPOSITE PAGE ABOVE: Two women model post office uniforms – the inclusion of a trousered uniform was hailed as a first.

OPPOSITE PAGE BELOW LEFT: Offering comfort and refreshments to children being evacuated by train.

OPPOSITE PAGE BELOW RIGHT: Women sort parcels at Mount Pleasant Post Office, Christmas 1940.

ABOVE: 'The tricycle girls start out on a day's work.' These women are delivering towels to City offices.

ABOVE INSET: A postwoman delivers the Christmas mail. Women were employed to help with the increased mail. They were not given uniforms but wore their own clothes.

OPPOSITE PAGE: By September 1941 many women were full employees of the Post Office, and this woman makes the afternoon collection from a City postbox.

Munitions workers

The production of munitions included not only the building of war machinery but also the manufacture of bombs, shells, mines and bullets used by that machinery. Hundreds of women were employed in producing the casings for these items, a task which involved working with smelting furnaces and hot metal. Once cast, the casings were sent to be filled in other factories, usually sited out of town because of the risk of explosion. In order to minimise this risk, women working with explosives wore a cloak and beret of undyed silk and rubber galoshes, and had to remove jewellery, corsets, hairpins or anything metal which might cause a spark.

ABOVE: Manufacturing 'Sten' guns at the Royal Ordnance factory in Theale, Berkshire.

ABOVE RIGHT: One of ninety training at the Beaufoy Institute in Lambeth, this young woman is learning how to use measuring calipers. The women had all paid £1 2s 2d (about £1.11) for a twelve-week course.

OPPOSITE PAGE ABOVE: Miss Josephine De La Porte, an evacuee from Jersey, is pictured making shells at a munitions factory.

OPPOSITE PAGE BELOW: 'Girl workers in the Bottling Department showing the shells being shaped and laid out to cool.'

A million women needed

RIGHT: Sewing soldiers' caps at a London clothing factory.

BELOW: 'Making the gun to shoot down the hun. Girls checking cannon-shell bodies–work particularly suitable for the defter fingers of the fairer sex.'

OPPOSITE PAGE TOP: Women work on one section of the production line of a factory that produced 4500 battle-suits each week.

OPPOSITE PAGE MIDDLE: These women work as cobblers, studding and toe-plating soldiers' boots.

OPPOSITE PAGE BELOW RIGHT: 'The Bomb Girls. In the front rank of the "out to win the war" girls are those hard at work turning out the bombs which are being used by the RAF to give the enemy a taste of what the people of Britain have experienced. They are being turned out in all kinds of buildings, from arsenals to large sheds which have been converted into miniature factories. Ex-waitress Miss Lilian Nye hauls a 500lb bomb.'

OPPOSITE PAGE BELOW RIGHT: This picture of a woman working on a shell case at a factory in southern England was used to help promote Winston Churchill's call for a million women to help with war work.

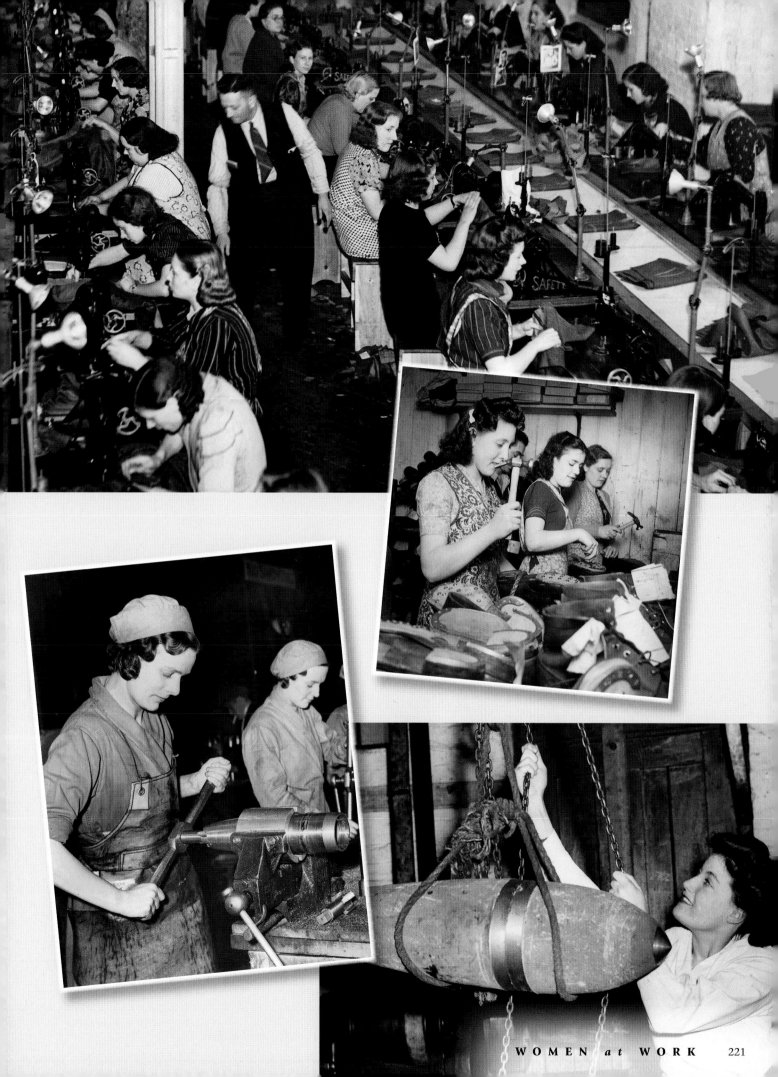

Working conditions

Even though women daily proved their abilities in the workforce, they were paid considerably less than their male counterparts. The average woman's pay in 1943 was £3 2s 11d, just over 50 per cent of the £6 1s 4d that was the average male pay. Additionally, working conditions were often very basic. As munitions factories were those converted from peacetime production, or were hastily converted or constructed buildings, and many of the machine tools were used for jobs for which they were not initially intended, safety was frequently a serious concern. Many factories were designed for men and far fewer workers than employed during the war, so that facilities like toilets and rest rooms were in short supply. Normal working hours were long and when there were calls for increased production, such as after the retreat from Dunkirk, the working day could be extended, so that women found themselves working from 8 a.m. to 7 p.m.

OPPOSITE PAGE: 'Women help in the high speed ship production in British shipyards. Women are now fast taking their places with the men in the yards, painting, plate marking, and generally carrying out tasks which before the war were considered hard even for the men. Miss Louisa Lines, aged 20, formerly a Yorkshire cotton machinist, painting along the scuppers of a nearly finished merchant ship.'

OPPOSITE PAGE INSET TOP: Touching up the coachwork of a plane before the engine is fitted.

OPPOSITE PAGE INSET BELOW: Mrs Eileen Glassett, here drilling wing spars for a Halifax bomber, had been a sales assitant in a womenswear shop in London's West End. Like many women she gave up her peacetime job to go into the factories.

ABOVE: The NAAFI canteen at a Royal Artillery unit in Cheshire.

BELOW RIGHT: Miss Elizabeth William, a former radio worker, operates a drill in an aircraft factory.

BELOW LEFT: Miss Pamela Anderson serves two ATS at a services canteen in St Martin-in-the-Fields Church.

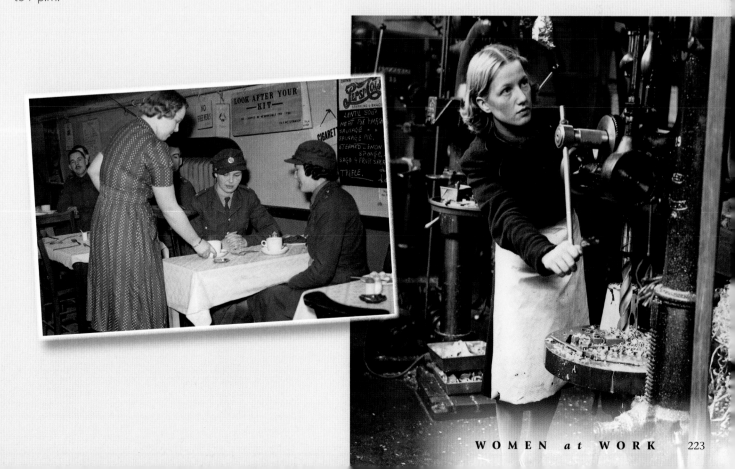

Heavy work

LEFT TOP: In January 1941, Britain's first dustwomen assumed their roles in Ilford. The council employed 'eight comely dustbin-emptiers'.

BELOW LEFT: 'Mrs Flannigan, a woman bricklayer, works to repair bomb damage to a Southern Railway arch in London.'

BELOW RIGHT: Two women install a gas cooker. At the gas works, women took on a range of jobs, from installation and maintenance of appliances to heavy labouring jobs such as filling 100-ton coke sacks.

OPPOSITE PAGE TOP: 'Women in the "Pick and Shovel Brigade". At a new aerodrome somewhere in East Anglia about 100 women and girls are doing navvies' work with zest and enjoyment. Here they are laying pipes for drainage each side of the runway.'

OPPOSITE PAGE BELOW RIGHT: 'She-navvies cheerfully wheel barrow loads of heavy stones at a railway goods yard. Women can no longer be called the "weaker sex" for all over Britain they have answered the call and taken on jobs which were previously exclusive to men. The toughest of these is surely that of "Women Navvies" a classification which includes a multitude of rough, heavy or dirty jobs.'

OPPOSITE PAGE BELOW LEFT: These women, here filling sandbags, were the first to be employed to clear air-raid debris and help make buildings safe.

'Land Girls'

Food production was another area that needed to recruit a large workforce. The Women's Land Army, members of which were nicknamed 'Land Girls', formed the backbone of the body of women engaged in the cultivation of the land and rearing of meat. Many other women factory workers, along with schoolchildren, the forces and men in reserved occupations, helped out on the land by taking advantage of schemes that gave a holiday on a farm in return for a payment of several hours' labour.

ABOVE: One of 'three girls of the Women's Land Army ploughing reclaimed land on a farm in Bedford, with the aid of three tractors working in echelon.'

RIGHT: This picturegraph was distributed by the Ministry Of Information in 1944. The statistics show that more workers were needed on the land than before the war. This was because Britain had to produce more of its own food and, as a result, 200 per cent more land was brought into production.

OPPOSITE PAGE TOP: In 1944, a Land Girl ploughs a field in southern England, wearing a tin helmet to protect her from the debris from flying bombs brought down by RAF fighters.

OPPOSITE PAGE BELOW RIGHT: Land Girls Margaret Gower and Mary Rigg (with 'Doodlebug' painted on her helmet) shelter from an overhead battle to bring down flying bombs.

OPPOSITE PAGE BELOW LEFT: Daisy Beales, a farmer's daughter, clears land with a billhook.

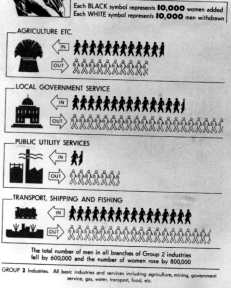

The part played by women in Britain's war effort

REPLACING MEN

4 examples from Group 2 Industries

Each BLACK symbol represents 10,000 women added
Each WHITE symbol represents 10,000 men withdrawn

AGRICULTURE ETC.

LOCAL GOVERNMENT SERVICE

PUBLIC UTILITY SERVICES

TRANSPORT, SHIPPING AND FISHING

The total number of men in all branches of Group 2 industries fell by 600,000 and the number of women rose by 800,000

GROUP 2 Industries. All basic industries and services including agriculture, mining, government service, gas, water, transport, food, etc.

Voluntary work

Many women who took on paid war work, part- or full-time, also took on voluntary work. This took various forms. Most voluntary work was organised through established groups like the Women's Institute, Women's Voluntary Service, Red Cross, Salvation Army and Church Army which were all well used to supporting and helping people with practical aid. They offered immediate tea and sympathy to air-raid victims as well as longer-term support for anyone in need. Several of these voluntary bodies also organised collections of materials for the war effort, jam making and rosehip picking, as well as promoting 'make do and mend' ideas and ways to make the most of the food rations. More unusual forms of voluntary work took the form of schemes such as those that saw office workers taking on a Sunday shift at a local factory to enable production to continue seven days a week.

LEFT: Dispensing articles from a 'Knitted Comforts Fund'. Knitting items for the troops was a way in which girls and women of all ages could make a voluntary contribution to the war effort.

OPPOSITE PAGE BELOW LEFT: A woman voluntary worker sorts some of the hundreds of packs of playing cards, woollens and footballs sent for the men of the British Expeditionary Force in the first few months of the war.

OPPOSITE PAGE BELOW RIGHT: A member of the Women's Voluntary Service cuts the hair of pensioner Mr W. H. Skipper at Woodford in Essex.

BELOW LEFT: 'Miss F. Stanley Hobart, General Montgomery's niece, drives a Church Army mobile canteen which serves troops with refreshments as well as offering military-style hair cuts.'

BELOW RIGHT: Women volunteers sort airgraph letters bound for the forces serving in the Middle East. The letters will be photographed and sent on a 100-foot spool of film to minimise the weight; at 6 ounces the film is more than 40 times lighter than 1500 letters.

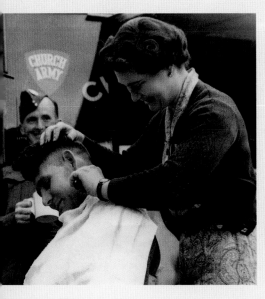

Working all hours

Women who did 'go into the factories' or into any other work during the war found time short and their lives burdened. Women with a home to keep were hit particularly hard. Compulsory overtime meant working hours were long, with half-day working on Saturday. Shops were closed by the time work finished; the working housewife had to shop in her lunch hour. Queuing for everything took time and the lack of facilities for keeping food fresh meant shopping regularly. Sunday was often the only day off in which to do the household chores, usually without the benefit of any mechanical aids.

Nevertheless, despite the difficulties of managing a home, a family and a job in which the pay and conditions were often demoralisingly low, the women of Britain responded enthusiastically to the demands and problems created by the war. Absentee rates were lower than before the war and production rates were met in full, often by women working beyond their compulsory hours to get the job done.

BELOW: Women of the Voluntary Ambulance Service take part in a military procession.

OPPOSITE PAGE TOP: A volunteer from the YMCA carries on serving refreshments during an air raid on Dover.

OPPOSITE PAGE MIDDLE RIGHT: After a performance, actresses Dorothy Haley Bell and Kay Astor, from the cast of *Tony Draws a Horse*, get ready in the dressing room to take up duty as an ambulance driver and a nurse.'

OPPOSITE PAGE BELOW RIGHT: These women were employees of Cable and Wireless and were part of a new unit called 'Telecom' which was formed to aid communications.

OPPOSITE PAGE BELOW LEFT: A group of volunteer ambulance women prepare for a practice run from their station in north-west London.

OPPOSITE PAGE MIDDLE LEFT: During a demonstration of ARP resources and procedures, a female ARP warden attends to a minor injury.

ATELY &
IMMEDIATELY
ARRANGED.

AXA 910

In the early weeks of the war this garage proprietor ensured
the petrol supplies were safe from the bombing with a
liberal stacking of sandbags.

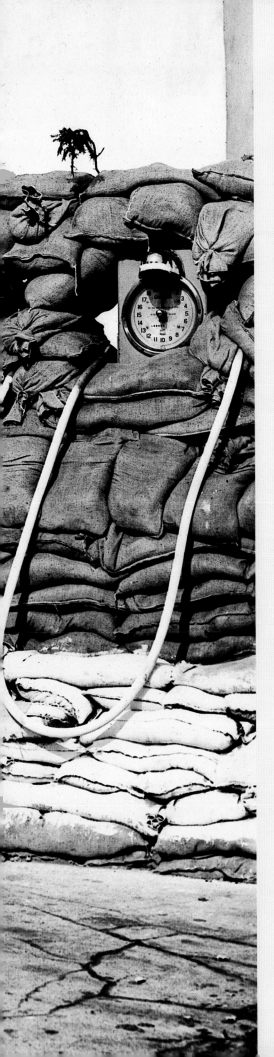

CHAPTER SIX

Working for the war effort

During the war, everyone, whether young or old, rich or poor, male or female, experienced at some stage, and to varying degrees, a life of unremitting toil, privation and loss. Complaints about conditions were frequently greeted with: 'Don't you know there's a war on!' The war effort required everyone's energy, through military service, paid employment, voluntary work or running a home. Through the effects of bombing, or the need to commandeer houses to accommodate military personnel or evacuees, some lost their homes and often their way of life. Everyone financed the war through their taxation and savings schemes which targeted everyone, even children. However, there was little to spend money on as there was insufficient spare manufacturing capacity in the country to produce luxury items, and imported goods and raw materials put the lives of merchant seamen at risk of attack from German battleships and U-boats.

Munitions

Once the government had established a military force, its next priority was to organise the production of the munitions with which that force could fight the war. Factory space, a labour force and raw materials were needed to produce munitions. Some raw materials were imported but many were provided by 'salvaging' or recycling items already in the country. Teams of women and children, organised by the Women's Voluntary Service (WVS), toured from house to house, collecting metal in the form of tin baths, saucepans and old tin cans. Additionally, they collected scrap rubber, rags, waste paper and old animal bones, all of which had some use in the production of weaponry.

OPPOSITE PAGE TOP: Inspecting shells at a Royal Ordnance factory. Quality control was very important in order to prevent the military being put at risk from its equipment.

OPPOSITE PAGE MIDDLE: Men at work in the torpedo workroom.

OPPOSITE PAGE BELOW: Inspection was carried out at all stages of production. Here the cases for naval shells are checked.

RIGHT TOP: Storing torpedoes in an Admiralty factory. Each torpedo contained more than 6000 parts and took several months to complete.

RIGHT BELOW: Every torpedo was 'tried out' and 'passed under working condition' before being dispatched to a Royal Navy ship.

Factory Force

Initially, factory space was provided by converting existing factories to munitions production. A few factories, such as Cadbury's Chocolate and Yardley Cosmetics, continued to run a small production line of their original products as morale boosters while the majority of the factory was turned over to the manufacturing of weapons. However, most factories converted wholly to munitions. As demand grew, many other buildings and premises were commissioned to serve as factories for the duration of the war. The haste of conversion from their original purpose meant that working conditions were rarely much more than basic.

OPPOSITE PAGE TOP LEFT: Signing on for the 'Munition Army' at Walworth Road Labour Exchange as part of the call for one million men to be registered.

OPPOSITE PAGE TOP RIGHT: Stockpiled shells photographed in November 1939. They were bound for the Belgian-French border where the British Expeditionary Force awaited a German offensive.

OPPOSITE PAGE BELOW: Shells arriving in the shell-inspecting shop at an ordnance factory.

RIGHT: Workmen stacking anti-aircraft shells.

BELOW: Shells being readied for transfer to the filling shops. Often ordnance produced in factories inside towns and cities were sent out of town to be filled with explosives. This reduced the risk of loss of life from explosions, caused either by enemy bombing or by accident.

Rifles

ABOVE LEFT: Rifles being stacked ready for dispatch. Photographed during the week of the retreat from Dunkirk, there was useful propaganda in ensuring that the public understood that, despite the fact that the soldiers had to leave most of their equipment behind, there were plenty more weapons in stock.

ABOVE RIGHT: Piling up rifles to service the British Expeditionary Force (BEF) in November 1939. The BEF had joined with French troops to prevent any further German advances.

LEFT: A factory inspecting room which was 'working at emergency pressure, day and night, to produce small arms, spare parts and tools.' Britain had not spent money on armaments in the years after the First World War and consequently when war broke out again it was a race to provide the equipment the military needed.

OPPOSITE PAGE: Thousands of empty cartridge cases ready for filling.

Speeding up production

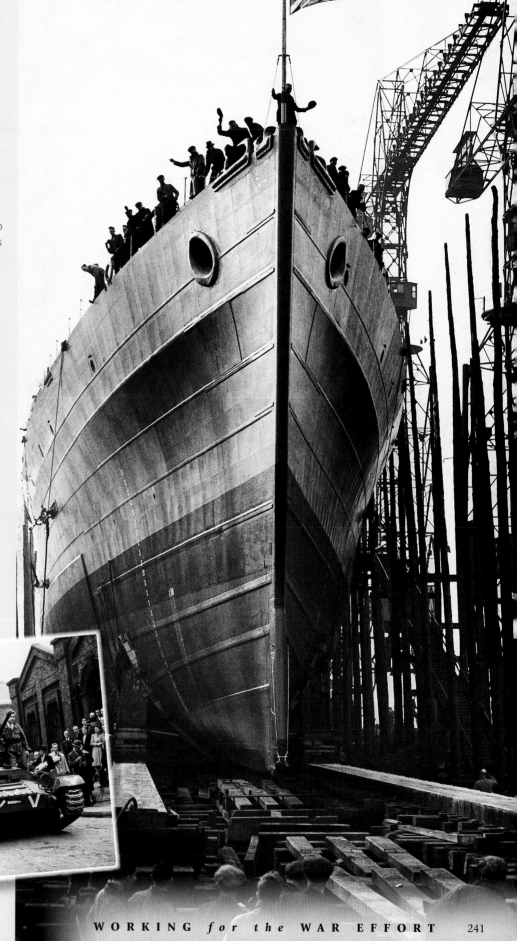

OPPOSITE PAGE TOP: A new production method to Britain, but one widely used in the USA, enabled the production of warships and merchant ships to be speeded up. The various parts of the ship were constructed at inland factories and then assembled on the slipway of the shipyard. This ship frame, photographed in September 1942, is one of the first built by this method.

OPPOSITE PAGE BELOW LEFT: Workers constructing a bulkhead for a merchant ship (in background). Britain's merchant fleet was vital in keeping the country supplied with food and raw materials. At this stage of the war, 1942, Britain was launching a 10,000-ton merchant ship every three weeks; this yard had the target of constructing 16 ships in the year.

OPPOSITE PAGE BELOW RIGHT: A newly built 8000-ton new warship is pulled by tugs into the fitting-out basin for the final touches before it assumes active service.

RIGHT: This warship gliding down the slipway was a product of Britain's one-a-week ship construction programme. As soon as it cleared the slipway the workers would start preparing the berth for the keel-plate of the next ship.

BELOW: Britain produced military hardware, like these tanks, not only for itself but also for allies such as Russia, which joined the forces against Hitler in June 1941 after a German attack on the USSR.

Building bombers

LEFT: A production line for the Blenheim bomber, 'whose speed and range', it was claimed, had 'outclassed anything the Germans have'. This was just one of the several aircraft factories around Britain producing fighter and bomber planes.

RIGHT: 'Your flying saucepan is doing just fine. The thousands of tons of aluminium pans that housewives gave up to the Ministry of Aircraft Production are making first-rate Spitfires. Smelting factories where saucepans, preserving pans and kettles are being turned into ingots for the plane factories are working at full pressure. Men, stripped to the waist, work in an atmosphere as warm as Kew Gardens' hothouse. Day and night, and through air raid warning, they shovel your household ware into furnaces and it comes out a flowing, white-hot liquid. The photo shows men stacking pure ingots of aluminium to dispatch to the Aircraft Presses.'

BELOW: Anti-aircraft guns on the production line in a Midlands factory.

ONE MONTH'S RATION FOR FOUR PEOPLE— ONE OVER 70 AND TWO CHILDREN.

EXTRA RATION

MARGARINE 4 lb.

LARD 2 lb.

BUTTER 2 lb.

SWEETS 1 lb.

EXTRA RATION

MARGARINE 2 lb.

TEA ¼ lb.

EXTRA RATION

TEA 2 lb.

SUGAR 8 lb.

We regret that the food Regulations do not permit the sale at this branch of Rationed Goods (other than Cooked Ham) to Customers registered at other Sainsbury branches.

NEWCASTLE CO-OPERATIVE SOCIETY LIMITED

Name ....
Address ....
....
Pass Book No. ....
Number in Household.................................

C.P.S. N/c

	WEEK ENDING:							
	Nov. 11th	Nov. 18th	Nov. 25th	Dec. 2nd	Dec. 9th	Dec. 16th	Dec. 23rd	Dec. 30th
BUTTER..								
BACON or HAM ..								
SUGAR ..								
....								
....								
....								

On the ration

OPPOSITE PAGE TOP: As early as January 1940 the first food rationing came into effect. This photograph does not represent all of the ration, as fresh milk and meat were also rationed. Foods such as bread, fish, offal and fruit were 'off the ration' but they were often in short supply.

OPPOSITE PAGE BELOW LEFT: As the war progressed more types of food were rationed. On 8th February 1943, tinned fruit came under the 'points' system which allowed people to purchase items, most often those deemed luxuries, in addition to the basic ration. There was some choice, for example tinned plums instead of tinned peaches, but there were still restrictions on the amount one could purchase.

OPPOSITE PAGE MIDDLE RIGHT: Collating coupons for the second issue of ration books. 'Machines costing thousands of pounds were installed for the new printing. The coupons were printed on strips of paper 8 in. wide. The full run of 50,000,000 books used 35,000 miles of it.'

OPPOSITE PAGE BELOW RIGHT: Staff in the Money Order Department at the GPO (Post Office), where the savings of millions of people were administered.

ABOVE: This shop assistant cuts the coupons from his customer's ration book. As the sign on the shelf states, it was only possible to buy rationed goods in the shop with which you were registered.

ABOVE INSET: This 'ration book', issued to members of the Newcastle Co-operative Society in November 1939, before official rationing, was probably a response to shortages. Butter, bacon, ham and sugar, the first items to be rationed when the official system came into effect, are the focus of this rationing system.

Coupons for food

ABOVE: People with surnames beginning with 'A' wait patiently to register for new ration books at the Fulham Food Office.

LEFT: A grocer cuts coupons from the ration book of Miss Ella White of Baker Street. There was much debate when ration books were first introduced as to whether they should have perforated sheets of coupons.

BELOW: Shopkeepers had to use scissors to cut out the coupons, which were about the size of a postage stamp or smaller.

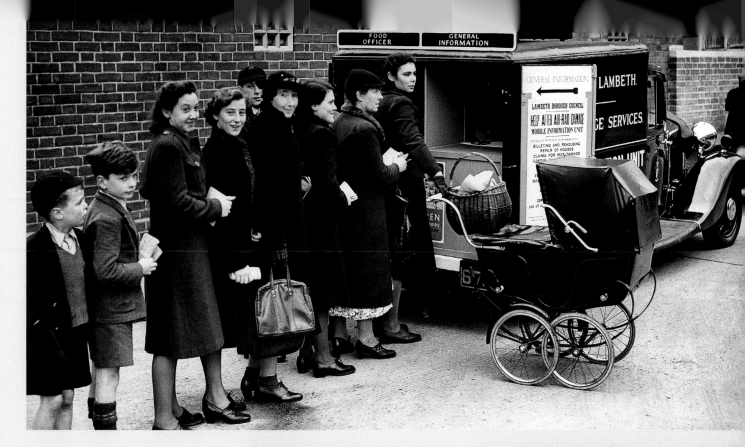

American generosity

RIGHT: Mothers at the Tottenham Welfare Centre receive bottles of concentrated orange juice for their children. The juice was newly arrived from the USA as part of the Lend-Lease Agreement. This picture was taken at the request of the USA's Department of Agriculture to promote the scheme and publicise American generosity.

ABOVE: A mobile van distributes new coupon books in an attempt to relieve the congestion at the Food Office. There was an added advantage in that it allowed more flexibility for working people to be able to collect their coupons.

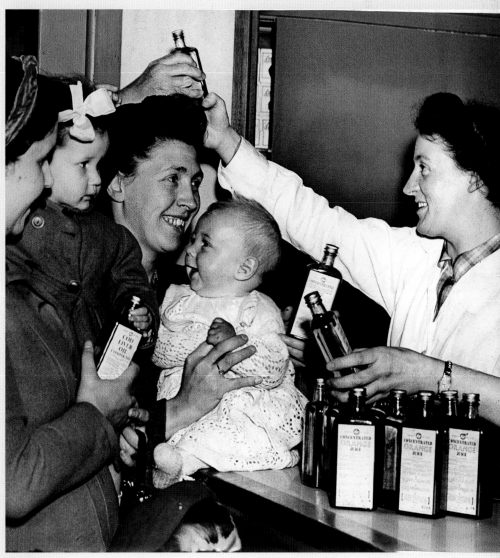

Making do

Food, clothes and petrol were all rationed; even soap was rationed and no one was allowed to have a bath more than five inches deep, in order to conserve fuel and the pressure on the water systems. If something was not rationed then the chances were that it was in short supply or simply unobtainable. People had to 'make do and mend', rescuing worn or broken items, and find inventive solutions to replace those items in short supply – constructing a baby's cot out of an old drawer, experimenting with mixtures of face cream and shoe polish to colour stockingless legs, making children's clothes out of cut-down adult clothing.

LEFT TOP: In June 1941 clothing rationing was introduced, using a points system. Originally 60 points per year were allocated to eveyone to be spent as wished. Later the points allocation was reduced to 48. Selfridges responded to the news of clothing rationing by setting up an enquiry desk to help answer customers' queries.

LEFT: A customer buys shirts with margarine coupons which, when clothes were first rationed, could be used if the buyer had not been issued with a clothing ration book.

OPPOSITE PAGE TOP: Choosing a suit where the number of coupons required is displayed more prominently than the price.

OPPOSITE PAGE BELOW: Crowds gather outside a shop window to see the 'coupon cost' of clothes on the first day of the scheme.

Life's luxuries

LEFT TOP: When clothes were first rationed, buying 30 pairs of stockings would have used up an entire year's clothing ration.

LEFT MIDDLE: Even before clothing rationing was introduced silk stockings were in short supply and this trader in Lambeth Walk has a crowd of customers for his wares.

LEFT BELOW: Women relax in the park, trying to acquire a suntan, which offered an alternative way to make legs look attractive when stockings were strictly rationed.

BELOW: During lunchtime in a City office one woman paints the legs of another with flesh-coloured paint, adding the finishing touch of a seam when the leg is covered.

OPPOSITE PAGE TOP: There was also a shortage of cigarettes and tobacco. Selfridges split their permitted deliveries into smaller batches to ensure a steady service to customers.

OPPOSITE PAGE BELOW: Men queue to buy cigarettes from a London kiosk.

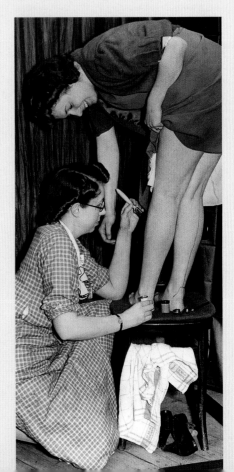

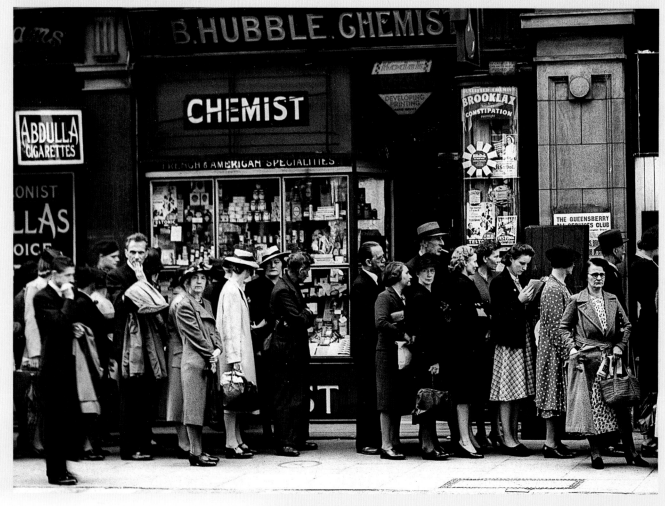

Queues for everything

As everything was in short supply people spent hours queuing for food and goods. The government controlled prices in an attempt to avoid profiteering. Some shopkeepers kept unrationed items 'under the counter' to sell only to regular customers. There was also a black market, which was illegal and often involved those who had been on the wrong side of the law before the war.

OPPOSITE PAGE TOP LEFT: 'At 9.00 a.m. she joins the queue for sausages. The "joint" has of course long disappeared and something must be found for lunch. The sausages are not yet in, but early queuing is necessary.'

OPPOSITE PAGE TOP RIGHT: '9.15. It's stopped raining, but it's hot and the very "flat" atmosphere is very tiring, so her coat comes off; something more to carry on her arms.'

OPPOSITE PAGE BELOW: In July 1942 a queue forms outside a sweet shop near Leicester Square as people try to stock up before sweets are rationed.

ABOVE: A queue in Kentish Town for the greengrocer's in July 1945. Despite the victory in Europe there was no sign of an improvement in supplies.

LEFT TOP: Queuing for fish in Streatham High Road in July 1945.

LEFT BELOW: A fish queue in Hammersmith in June 1945. The fishmonger was able to supply the fish but customers had to bring their own paper in which to wrap it.

An anti-queue movement

While it was a constant effort to obtain food, and women in paticular spent hours queuing for food, many experts now claim that, as the standard food ration was calculated by nutritionists, during the war people were better fed than at any time before or since.

Women also had to spend time cooking, or learning to cook, some things they would never have dreamt of serving before the war – sheep's head, carrot marmalade, fruit cakes made with dried eggs and grated beetroot, 'banana' sandwiches made from parsnips flavoured with artificial banana flavouring. Bananas were unavailable for most of the war and the few imported oranges were reserved for children. People spent hours labouring in their gardens or allotments as part of the 'Dig for Victory' campaign to supplement the family's diet with fresh home-grown produce.

OPPOSITE PAGE TOP: This is a queue for ice cream, a luxury item, although the product these women are queuing for probably contained no cream, being made from dried milk powder, dried egg, water and flavourings. The energy required to freeze it would be sufficient to make it a luxury.

OPPOSITE PAGE BELOW: Queuing for tomatoes at a Birmingham greengrocer's soon after VE Day, when there was a developing movement to try to do something about the endless queuing.

ABOVE: A week after the devastating raid on Coventry in November 1940, people queue for water from a standpipe.

RIGHT: Women from the Salvation Army make notes at an 'anti-queue' meeting in the Waldorf Hotel between the National Council for Women and the Council of Retail Distributors.

Working for the war effort

Working hours were long. The normal working week was eight hours Monday to Friday and four hours on a Saturday, but most employees worked at least a 10-hour day as they were required for compulsory overtime. Once a work shift was over there were other demands on an individual's time. Many workers also contributed their service to the Home Guard or the ARP service. Some people with office jobs during the week worked on Sundays in factories which ran production lines 24 hours a day, seven days a week. This enabled the factory workers to have at least one clear day off. Thousands of others 'lent a hand on the land' during their spare time, taking holidays on farms, helping to plant or gather the harvest. Women workers also had the demands of running a home, trying to shop in their lunchtimes, cooking and cleaning in their precious hours at home.

ABOVE: A mobile unit from the National Emergency Washing Service, which provided free clothes washing for those without access to washing facilities, because they had been either bombed out of their homes or evacuated to safer areas.

LEFT: An emergency 'Food Office' for those whose homes suffered damage in raids by V1 bombs. The office replaced the ration books of those who had lost them in the bombing.

OPPOSITE PAGE TOP: 'A Ministry of Food "Flying Squad" at work soon after a "flying bomb" had fallen in Southern England. A Marquee and field kitchen were set up for supplying hot meals.'

OPPOSITE PAGE BOTTOM: Emergency food vans such as this one, a gift from the car magnate Henry Ford, toured bombed areas dispensing cooked food.

Fuel rationing

ABOVE LEFT: Vehicle fuel was reserved for the military and other transport necessary to the war effort. It was only available to members of the public for 'essential' journeys – a doctor doing his rounds in a rural area, for example. Most cars were out of action for the duration of the war.

ABOVE RIGHT TOP: Apart from a few buses for late-night workers, a 10.00 p.m. curfew was imposed on London's buses. Although the main reason was to preserve lives during the Blitz, it had the added advantage of saving fuel.

ABOVE RIGHT BELOW: In response to the lack of petrol for motorised taxis, an old fashioned 'growler' cab, driven by horse power, made an appearance on London's streets.

LEFT MIDDLE AND BELOW: Increasing numbers of horses were seen on Britain's roads for all manner of jobs, mainly transporting goods.

OPPOSITE PAGE TOP: 'With petrol rationing and motorists laying up their cars, horses are coming into their own again. And street scenes resembling more and more those of days gone by. Compare this picture in Piccadilly yesterday (5th October 1939) with the scene in 1891 (inset right).'

OPPOSITE PAGE BELOW: 'First day of petrol rationing (25th September 1939) – and this was the scene yesterday on a by-pass road near London which is usually crowded with speeding cars. People ambled pleasantly on horseback or bicycled gaily by, but for the greater part of the day there was not a car to be seen.'

Coal supplies

Coal was the most essential fuel during the war. It powered the electricity stations, was important in the production of gas, was needed for smelting metal for munitions and was the chief source of domestic heating. Ensuring supplies of coal throughout the war was always a problem. With around three million working men in the forces, it was important to have enough labour to produce the weapons they needed. Men not eligible for active duty were redirected into war work; both men and women were conscripted into war work. The most notable of these were the 'Bevin Boys' – from December 1943 one in ten of newly conscripted men were selected by ballot to work in the coal mines. Other workers, such as farmers and train drivers, came under an Essential Work Order and were not required to undertake military service as their skills and experience were vital to keeping the country running smoothly. They could not be sacked and were not permitted to move to another job.

ABOVE: Keeping coal supplies close to where they would be used helped avoid congestion on the rail network at peak times of demand. Here Marylebone Borough Council store coal for the winter at a bomb-damage site in Baker Street.

BELOW: Coal dumps ran a cash-and-carry scheme whereby local people could visit, pay for coal and take it away with them.

OPPOSITE PAGE: This notice informs residents that, due to a shortage of coal in southern England, the emergency coal dumps would be closed down.

Every ounce counts

LEFT: 'Westminster City Council have put galvanised bins at street corners. Notices on the covers tell housewives what they should put in the bins to help feed pigs and other livestock on our farms.'

BELOW: The Women's Land Army making hay on Arlington Manor Farm, Guildford, in the summer of 1942. The WLA was formed in response to the shortage of 100,000 farm labourers and the need for Britain to produce more of its food at home.

OPPOSITE PAGE TOP: 'Land Girls' feeding pigs. 'Land Girls' was the soubriquet of the Women's Land Army, which proved to be a vital source of agricultural workers.

OPPOSITE PAGE MIDDLE AND BELOW: Land Girls stooking and gathering the sheaves on a farm in Buckinghamshire in the summer of 1944, by which time the WLA numbered 80,000.

CITY OF WESTMINSTER
WANTED
SCRAPS for VEGETABLES and SALADS
MEAT FISH and BREAD
POTATO and APPLE PEEL
NOT WANTED
RUBBER TEA LEAVES
COFFEE GROUNDS
SKINS of GRAPE FRUIT
ORANGES LEMONS and BANANAS
GREY SOAP and SODA

PLACE YOUR FOOD WASTE HERE

EVERY OUNCE COUNTS

Financial contribution

The citizens of Britain contributed to the war effort with their labour in the factories and fields, their time, their household items, their creativity and their spirit. However, they also made a huge financial contribution. The War Budget in September 1939 raised taxation to 7s 6d (37p) in every pound, raised again in 1941 to 10s (50p). Surprisingly, even with this tax rate, many people had money to spare, generated from overtime pay and the fact that many families had at least one more income than before the war. However, there was little to spend it on and the government needed money to finance the war. That money came from people's spare cash in the form of war savings, which were promoted aggressively, and savings groups organised in factories, offices and even schools.

LEFT TOP: Soldiers help gather the harvest in 1941. After the retreat from Dunlirk there was little active fighting to be done, as Britain gathered its forces for an invasion of Hitler's 'Fortress Europe'.

LEFT BELOW: Children evacuated to south Wales help with the potato harvest.

OPPOSITE PAGE: Workers from Ilford shoulder their forks and march to their allotments.

OPPOSITE PAGE INSET: Women from Peckham, evacuated with their babies, work on a farm at Bromley Common.

Dig for victory

TOP: The development of allotments was encouraged and by 1943 there were 1,400,000. Additionally, parks and open spaces were turned over to growing food; golf clubs, tennis courts, grass verges and the moat of the Tower of London were all utilised. Here a Mr and Mrs Flack 'dig for victory' on Clapham Common.

ABOVE LEFT: Maureen Copeland helps her dad prepare the soil on their plot on Clapham Common.

ABOVE RIGHT: Winifred Chapman shoulders her spade, ready to work on Clapham Common.

OPPOSITE PAGE TOP: Britain needed to be able to produce as much food as possible and the 'Dig for Victory' campaign encouraged people to grow their own. Often this would provide the majority of a family's fresh fruit and vegetables. Here schoolchildren in Monmouthshire tend vegetables in the school garden.

OPPOSITE PAGE BELOW: For many families with men away in the forces it was not possible to keep an allotment. Mrs Mann and Mrs Padwick, pictured here surveying the allotments in Hyde Park, were just such cases. Produce of other allotment workers' labour would contribute to the diet of these families.

Changed landscapes

By the end of the war Britain looked very different. Six years of war had scarred many of its most beautiful buildings and the landscape had changed as more and more of its acreage had been brought into production. People too looked different; many were worn out after years of hard work and worry and were dressed in either uniform or old and worn or 'utility' style clothing. Life seemed dull and dreary, with shortages of even the most basic household items and a diet that was nutritionally sound but very limited in range.

LEFT TOP: A worker tends crops within sight of the Albert Memorial in Kensington Gardens.

LEFT MIDDLE: 'London of 1941. Park Lane, London's most expensive residential district provides us with the perfect allotment for the benefit of those "Digging for Victory". Women taking notes from the gardener who is giving hints as to the best way of producing vegetables.'

LEFT BELOW: In response to pleas to stay at home over the holiday period so that the railway lines would be left clear for urgent war transport, these people tend their allotments during Easter 1942.

OPPOSITE PAGE TOP: Hurlingham Polo Club gave over its grounds to Fulham Borough Council for use as allotments.

OPPOSITE PAGE BELOW: 'There is a prosperous farm about a quarter of an acre in extent, tucked away under the shadow of St Giles, Cripplegate, which was damaged in the 1940 air raids. Firemen from the station across the way made it, almost everything there, except the livestock, was provided by the blitz. The bricks for the pigsties came from bombed buildings, so does the wood from which the fowl-houses and the "tomatory" are made. On it there are almost every vegetable known to gardeners, and six apple trees, reputed to be the only apple trees in the City.'

CHAPTER SEVEN

Growing up at war

For many children the six years the war lasted encompassed the bulk of their childhood. Paradoxically, while it was a time of danger and fear, of dislocation and loss, it was also a time of unprecedented freedom for many children, and the community spirit arising from the privations of war made them feel secure. Children were also encouraged to contribute to the war effort, and did so in many important ways.

Early evacuees

Images of evacuation are those that spring most readily to mind when we think about children during the war years. Even before war was declared, the official evacuation schemes began. As part of the process, Britain was divided into three sorts of areas: evacuation, reception and neutral. Evacuation areas were those in danger of bombing, principally in large cities and areas of industrial production. Reception areas were situated in country towns and villages considered safe; here people were expected to offer billets to those from evacuation areas. No one could leave, or be evacuated to, neutral areas.

ABOVE: Carefully carrying their gas masks, these East End schoolchildren leave for their evacuation destinations on the day before war was declared. Some parents had taken the decision to evacuate their children privately – often abroad to places like Canada. However, the official evacuation did not begin until 30th August 1939.

ABOVE INSET: Evacuees board a bus at Edgware Station on 1st September 1939. Although still officially the summer holidays, children reported to school. They left with only the belongings they could carry, labelled and accompanied by teachers.

RIGHT: 'The Lost Worshippers. This picture was taken yesterday at a church a few yards from the London school bombed in the day raid last week. A week before nearly 200 attended the service. Now the pews are empty but for a few children who survived the Luftwaffe's attack.'

OPPOSITE PAGE TOP: A convoy of buses on the Kingston bypass, carrying schoolchildren to a mainline station for evacuation by train.

OPPOSITE PAGE BELOW: Children asleep on the floor of their classroom. They had gathered there the previous day to be registered and processed. They slept overnight at school, ready for their evacuation journey the following day.

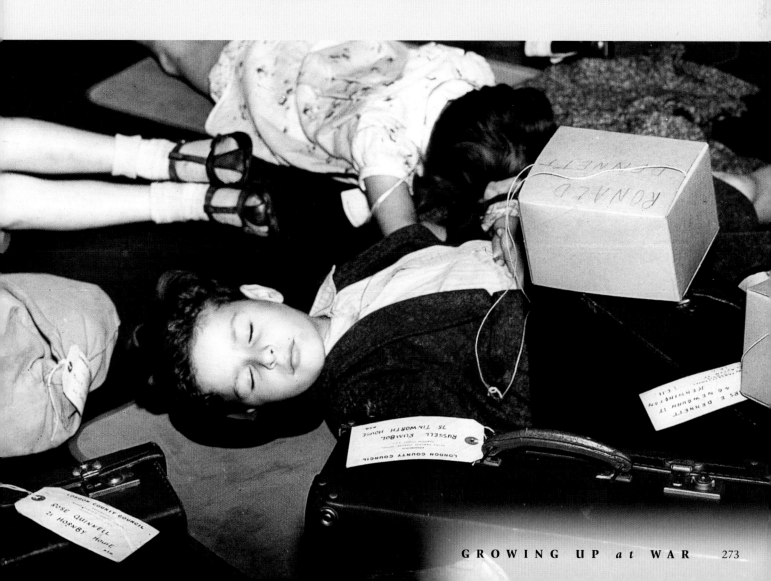

Seeking safety

In the first weeks of the war nearly four million people moved from evacuation to reception areas. These included pregnant women, mothers of pre-school children and disabled people, as well as school-age children. Throughout the war, evacuation schemes continued, with peak numbers related directly to the severity of the bombing. After the 'phoney war' of the first year, many children returned home, only to be re-evacuated when the Blitz began. Even before then, some children, evacuated to the south coast of England, had to be relocated when the area suffered attacks during the summer of 1940.

School-age children were evacuated without their parents. They were required to report to their school with only a change of clothes, basic toilet essentials, a packed lunch and, of course, a gas mask. At the school they were tagged with luggage labels, a precaution against children becoming lost but especially important for the youngest, who may not have known their address. Accompanied by teachers and helpers, the children were taken by buses and trains to the reception areas. Trips were as long as twelve hours; many children arrived exhausted by the journey, upset at leaving their parents and fearful of what life would be like in their new home.

OPPOSITE PAGE TOP: Despite the worries of evacuation, these younsters leaving London on 1st September 1939 are happy at the thought of 'a second holiday'.

OPPOSITE PAGE BELOW: In December 1939 the second official evacuation scheme started. These children reading the *Nipper* annual are part of a group leaving for Devon and the prospect of Christmas in new surroundings.

ABOVE: The retreat from Dunkirk in 1940 prompted more mass evacuations. These children sit patiently on a train at Paddington Station waiting for the start of the journey to their evacuation destination.

ABOVE MIDDLE: A group of children, part of the second wave of evacuation which relocated 10,000, pass through at Waterloo Station.

RIGHT: A cheery group on board the train during the second wave of evacuation.

Town meets country

Evacuation was the major impact of the war on many children's lives. Often the clash of cultures between children from the city and their hosts in the countryside was a source of problems for all concerned. Children from the poorest areas in the major cities frequently lived in deprived conditions, often without access to running water. Consequently, they were often unwashed and prone to minor infections such as scabies and impetigo. While this shocked many host families, most were understanding and worked hard to accept the evacuees into their homes. Sometimes the difference in standards was the other way round and children with baths and electric lights at home found themselves staying in farm labourers' cottages without running water or electricity.

OPPOSITE PAGE: This young Londoner, 'labelled and loaded', gets ready to leave for safety towards the end of the Blitz.

OPPOSITE PAGE INSET: A group of London schoolgirls off to billets in Monmouth and Glamorgan. They were part of a contingent of 10,000 children evacuated on one single day from London and the Medway towns.

ABOVE TOP: Children at Waterloo Station to catch a train to the West Country are escorted by police.

ABOVE INSET: 'The British lion took a bow at the train window yesterday when this party of schoolgirls were being evacuated from the South-East coast to the west of England.'

RIGHT: This young boy is on his way to the West Country, one of many children who were originally evacuated to the countryside of south-east England but were relocated when the area became vulnerable to attack.

Leaving London

ABOVE: 'Thumbs up' from these youngsters who were just a few of the 120,000 London children evacuated in June 1940.

RIGHT: These girls, survivors from a daylight bombing raid on their school in Catford, select books for their long evacuation journey. The attack on their school in January 1943 killed 23 children, a loss of life that caused much public anguish.

OPPOSITE PAGE: 'After the vicious Nazi attack on London last Wednesday (16th April 1941), all arguments against the evacuation of children have been settled in those areas badly blitzed, and nine times the usual number under the LCC evacuation scheme are now leaving London. An engine driver says "hello" to evacuees at a London station.'

Settling in to new homes

Having never before experienced the quietness, the solitude or the animal life of the countryside, some children found their new surroundings disturbing. Conversely, others found a freedom and enjoyment they had not experienced in urban life roaming rural lanes and fields. Almost all, whatever their circumstances, grew to hold their host families in affection and many formed relationships which continued long after life returned to 'normal'. On both sides, there was a determination to 'make things work'; a way of contibuting to the war effort.

OPPOSITE PAGE TOP: 'Children making their way up a hillside agleam with flowers.' Taken in the first week of the evacuation, this picture intended to show the experience of life in the reception areas.

OPPOSITE PAGE INSET: Pictured in September 1942, before leaving for their new billets, the King family, Allen, Roy, Doris and Lydia, were chosen as 'model' evacuees to promote evacuation schemes.

OPPOSITE PAGE BELOW: Smiling children used to promote the benefits of evacuation. Taken after the first evacuees left their homes, it was intended to reassure the parents left behind and to encourage more people in safe areas to offer billets to evacuees.

RIGHT TOP: A notice broadcasting to parents the safe arrival of their children to an evacuation area.

RIGHT MIDDLE: Boys from Dulwich College sort out their luggage on arrival at their evacuation school in Tonbridge in Kent.

BELOW: 'A day with the evacuated children in the country. East End children and others enjoying the sunshine in Berkshire, reading letters from home.'

A *new way* of life

RIGHT: These evacuees from a Dr Barnardo's Home in Middlesbrough were housed in Ripley Castle.

BELOW: These youngsters being read to by a nurse are evacuees from the Channel Islands, which were occupied by German troops at the end of June 1940. Although the government made a decision that the islands could not be defended, in the weeks prior to the invasion many people, and even livestock and crops, were evacuated. However, many other islanders had to live until August 1944 under German occupation.

OPPOSITE PAGE TOP: The boys' washroom at an evacuee camp near Farnham looks institutional. While every effort was made to billet evacuees in family homes, it was sometimes necessary for groups of schoolchildren to be billeted in camps.

OPPOSITE PAGE MIDDLE: Evacuees from Bow in London to a middle-class bungalow near Woking, these children would have found life very different from home.

OPPOSITE PAGE BELOW: Lord Blanesburgh listens to the evening radio broadcast of *Children's Hour* with the group of evacuees billeted in his stately home.

Life in the country

ABOVE: Miss Eileen Hocking shows Robert Yoghill and William Williams how to milk the cows. The boys, from London, were evacuated on to the Hocking family farm in Cornwall.

MIDDLE: Evacuees gaze into the village sweetshop in October 1940, a period when sweets were not yet rationed.

RIGHT: 'London kiddies evacuated to a little Welsh village are attending the village school. One of the most important lessons is the Welsh language instruction, for many of the villagers know no English.'

On the beach

ABOVE: Paddling in the sea around Britiain's coastal areas, as these evacuees are on 4th September 1939, soon became an impossibility.

RIGHT: As the beaches around Britain's shores were fortified against invasion with mines and barbed wire, children, like these boys, could only gaze longingly at the sea.

Reunited

OPPOSITE PAGE: Following weeks of separation since the children were evacuated to Saffron Walden from their home in Tottenham, the Elliott family were re-united in October 1939. Here, Mrs Elliott reserves a special hug for the youngest.

OPPOSITE PAGE INSET LEFT: Mrs Elliott runs to greet her six daughters.

OPPOSITE PAGE INSET RIGHT: The Elliott family are all together again.

RIGHT: A young girl searches her father's pockets for a treat in their first meeting for almost two months.

RIGHT INSET: In September 1944, these tired and weary travellers at Euston are part of the movement of returning evacuees. Unlike the coordinated and official process of evacuation, the return was much more low key. Families simply collected their evacuated children.

BELOW: The Good family returned to London after a five-year-long absence to find it much changed. Many families did not, or could not, return to their original homes but made a new life for themselves, often in areas to which they had been evacuated.

Back to school

One of the most enjoyable things for children about the start of the war was the fact that it extended the school summer holidays. Initially, the government announced an indefinite extension of the summer holidays but, by the middle of September, once the first evacuations were completed, most schools were reopened in the reception areas. It took slightly longer in the towns and cities; schools could only open once they had air-raid shelters and then could only teach the number of pupils they had shelter space for. The effect of this was part-time schooling – younger pupils being taught in the morning, older ones in the afternoon. A similar shift system was often found in the countryside as well, where the influx of evacuees usually meant that the village school could not accommodate all the children at once.

ABOVE RIGHT: The Headmistress at Mayville Road School in Leyton shows the infants the sandbagged trenches that were to provide shelter in the event of a raid.

RIGHT: Kennington Road Girls' School suffered during the Blitz and was hit by a flying bomb in 1944. Despite the obvious damage lessons carried on.

OPPOSITE PAGE TOP: Grange Park School, north London, reopened on 20th September, after an extra-long summer holiday. Children did not have to attend but most did.

OPPOSITE PAGE INSET MIDDLE: Canadian soldiers at a garden party in Surrey entertain young evacuees.

OPPOSITE PAGE INSET BELOW: Four energetic evacuees off for a dip.

Keeping them entertained

Although children were expected to make a contribution to the war effort, they also often had a good deal of time to fill. In the shelters there was little to occupy them apart from board games, cards or reading. The radio, or 'wireless', was the most popular form of entertainment, and programmes like *Children's Hour* were broadcast specially for children. Saturday-morning cinema was the other important source of entertainment. There was a special programme for children with short films and cartoons and an adventure serial such as *Tarzan*, *The Lone Ranger* or *Flash Gordon* that left the hero on a cliffhanger to encourage audiences back the next week.

OPPOSITE PAGE TOP: 'The mighty atom – the national savings campaign in schools.' Children were encouraged, like their parents, to contribute to the war effort by putting their money into National Savings. Here children in a Kent school line up to deposit their savings.

OPPOSITE PAGE BELOW LEFT: Boys of Eton College found the place changed when they returned from their summer vacation in 1939. Here three boys, carrying gas masks, examine the sandbagged entrance to an air-raid shelter.

OPPOSITE PAGE BELOW RIGHT: 'Waiting in the shelter with gas masks at the ready.'

RIGHT: Reading comics and singing songs, these children and their teachers entertain themselves while taking cover in the school shelter during an air-raid alarm.

BELOW: 'Boys of the Workington and Cumberland Technical and Secondary School who are in their final year help in the making of munitions by staying behind and working after school hours.'

Working hard

Children contributed a great deal to the war effort. They helped their parents in the 'Dig for Victory' campaign by working in their gardens or allotments. They were also able to 'lend a hand on the land' by joining teams working on farms to boost food production.

Many of the 'drives' co-ordinated by the Womens Volunteer Service (WVS) relied on children's help with picking wild fruits and plants such as blackberries, crab apples, mushrooms and dandelion leaves. In something of a virtuous circle, children were also part of the teams collecting wild rosehips, which volunteers turned into rosehip syrup, a rich source of vitamin C, which was then given to children.

The WVS also ran 'salvage' drives, collecting door-to-door unused household items and waste. Children were also essential members of these drives, which provided some of the raw material for munitions.

OPPOSITE PAGE TOP: Children from London take part in a National Day of Prayer before setting off to the fields to help with hop picking.

OPPOSITE PAGE BELOW: Schoolboys from Eton on 'Long Leave' tending the allotments of members of the Eton Working Men's Allotment Society.

BELOW: 'The heart of Britain. In the spirit of this picture, in blitzed Bristol, fair and historic city. In Bristol they have danced the May Dances, always, and amid the wrecked homes the children still dance the May-days, and their elders still watch them.'

BOTTOM RIGHT: Schoolboys in Essex examine incendiary bombs which fell in their school grounds.

BOTTOM LEFT: A Harrow School boy with some of his 'souvenirs', collected from the school grounds after raids during the Blitz.. Many children, especially boys, collected war 'souvenirs'. At Harrow, the boys traded them for money which was donated to the 'Spitfire Fund'.

Running free

Many children were out of school for long periods and often they were unsupervised at home because Father was with the forces or working, and Mother was working as well. This led to a number of social problems. For example, there was an increase in vandalism and hooliganism. Public air-raid shelters were wrecked so many times by children that in the end they had to be kept locked, opened by the ARP warden when the alert sounded.

However, many children just enjoyed the freedom from continual adult scrutiny. They were free to play imaginary games and collect war 'souvenirs'. Bits of bombs and crashed planes were collected from bomb and crash sites and traded among children. This obviously unsafe activity was discouraged in varying degrees by adults.

OPPOSITE PAGE: Four boys take tea in the garden of their damaged home after a daylight raid in March 1943.

OPPOSITE PAGE INSET: Children from a London orphanage survey the wreckage of their home after it was hit during the Blitz.

RIGHT ABOVE: The child at play on the home-made cart calmly reads the danger notice.

RIGHT: After a particularly heavy raid on Coventry in April 1941, these schoolboys are given refreshments from a mobile canteen donated by the Americans.

CITY OF LONDON POLICE
DANGER
UNEXPLODED
BOMB

U.S.A. TO BRITAIN. MIN OF

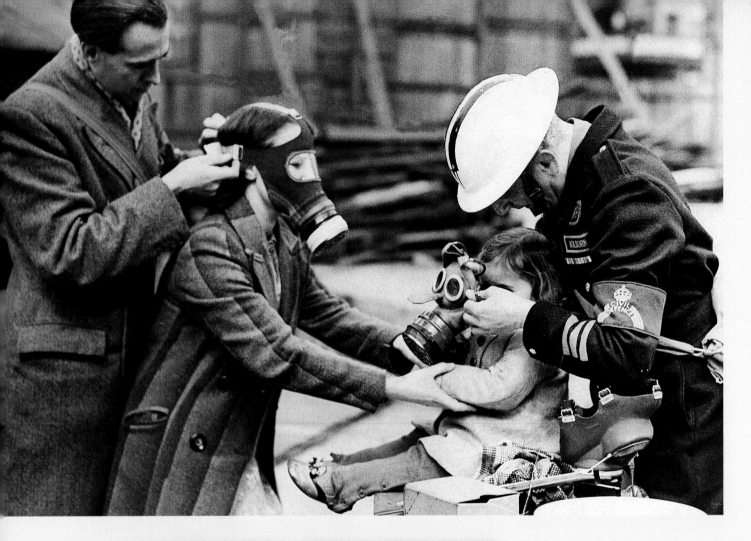

Protecting children

ABOVE: This little girl, Pat, was having her first gas mask fitted, comforted by her mother. Her red and blue mask had a 'nose' which made it look like the cartoon character Mickey Mouse.

LEFT: 'Wendy brings her gas mask to be repaired and points out the perished rubber and the small holes in the face piece.'

OPPOSITE PAGE TOP AND BELOW: In March 1941 there were concerns raised by the council in Dover suggesting an increase in the child population of the town. It is difficult to say whether this was a result of evacuee children in the area, or the fact that children had more free time and were less strictly supervised and so were more evident.

CHAPTER EIGHT

Business as usual

Although people on the home front lived
with the constant threat of invasion or aerial
attack and suffered the privations of rationing,
shortages and the blackout, there remained
a tremendous spirit in the British population.
That spirit manifested itself in a determination
to carry on as near as 'normal' a life as possible.
Early on in the war, the legend 'Business as Usual'
was seen chalked on many bombed-out shops;
it became a slogan for everyone.

Keeping up morale

The government capitalised on the positive public mood and boosted morale by promoted the idea of working together to defeat the enemy. Most propaganda campaigns emphasised social responsibility – 'Careless talk costs lives', 'Dig for victory', 'Women, join the factories', 'Do not waste food' – a far cry from the campaigns of the Great War which presented the Germans, or 'the Hun', as evil. Even simple things like donating pots, pans and garden railings to salvage drives encouraged the feeling of being able to contribute directly to the war effort.

More subtly, the presentation of attractive, glamorous young men and women working together in factories, army camps, airbases or on ships implied a British way of life under threat from Hitler and well worth protecting.

ABOVE: Capturing the humour of ordinary people, the notice painted on the side of this shelter suggests, perhaps ironically, that a night sheltering in an air raid is as entertaining as an evening in the music hall.

LEFT: The proprietor of this boot repair shop in Battersea was called up in the first week of the war and leaves a note for his customers on his plans for reopening.

OPPOSITE PAGE: This street fruit seller boasts that his oranges have come through Musso's (Mussolini's) 'Lake' – a nickname for the Mediterranean. He also has bananas for sale – a rarity during the war, especially by the time of the Blitz when this picture was taken.

'Keep smiling through'

Public morale was closely monitored. Without public support the prosecution of a war by a demoractic nation is difficult to sustain. Thus, there was government resistance when people first started sheltering in the Underground. Initially anxious to avoid a 'deep shelter mentality' in which fearful citizens spent all their time underground, the government eventually conceded when it was clear that this was not the case. Other government strategies, such as keeping in place production of items such as cosmetics and chocolate and sanctioning extra rations at special times like Christmas, kept morale high; in the words of Vera Lynn's song, the majority of the population did 'keep smiling through', often with comic good humour.

OPPOSITE PAGE TOP LEFT: 'An amusing offer seen in London after a bomb had demolished a dwelling house.'

OPPOSITE PAGE TOP RIGHT: Although a somewhat gruesome sight, this picture, taken in London towards the end of the Blitz, is a vivid demonstration of the of the fact that the severe bombing campaign had not brought about public pressure for the government to sue for peace with Germany.

OPPOSITE PAGE BELOW: 'British humour prevails through weeks of air raids: a comic police notice. Many street notices in London testify to the fact that in spite of the air raids British people are smiling through with characteristic humour. Here is a policeman's effort in the London area, warning passers-by to pass by quickly in a danger zone.'

RIGHT TOP: The signs on this ARP shelter offer a humourously defiant challenge.

RIGHT BELOW: An ironic message for the milkman from the residents of this Hackney street: 'Don't leave any milk'.

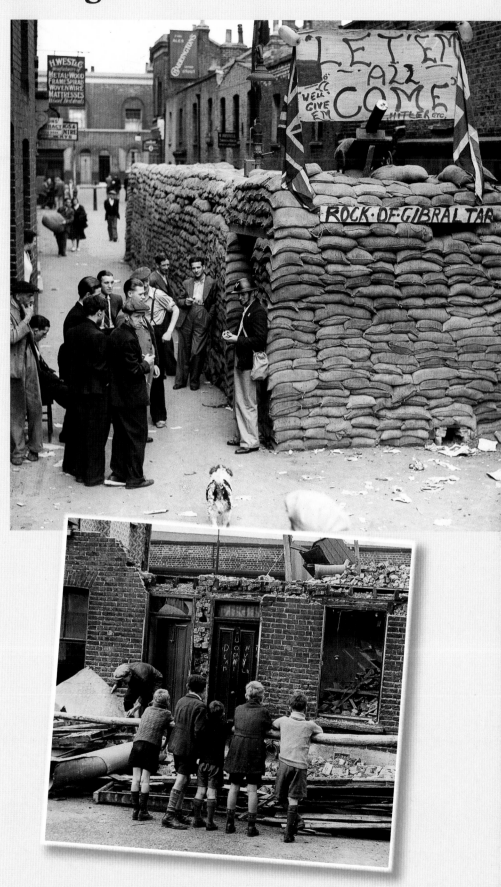

Life goes on

While there was tremendous pride in the idea of 'business as usual', there was an understanding that much had changed. Life went on but many of the pre-war social patterns had had to change in order to ensure that continuity. The pre-war bans on married women working were gone and women formed a huge percentage of the workforce. Class barriers began to break down as people shared experiences of evacuation, military service, sheltering during air raids and toil in the workplace. By 1944 a series of plans for radical changes to post-war society had been published, most notably plans for free secondary education and a National Health Service with the aim of giving everyone access to a good education and healthcare.

LEFT: This bomb-damaged shop in south-west London hangs out the Union Jacks and declares that it is still open for business.

OPPOSITE PAGE TOP: A hairdresser's in the West End of London after a raid sports the legend 'Business as Usual'.

OPPOSITE PAGE MIDDLE: A messenger puzzles out where to redirect his packages as the businesses to which he is delivering have been re-homed following the destruction of their original premises in one of the worst raids of the Blitz.

OPPOSITE PAGE BELOW: 'Methodically the German airmen hit hospitals whenever they manage to penetrate the London barrage, and when a bomb fell on this hospital last night a nurse was killed. Nevertheless, her comrades went immediately to work when daylight came to clear up.'

Entertainment

Entertainment was an important area for keeping up morale. When war was declared venues for public entertainment, such as cinemas, theatres, concert halls and football grounds, were closed down to avoid the possibility of many people being killed in a direct hit on a crowded area. When no bombing came many reopened with air-raid precautions in place.

Cinema was one of the most popular forms of public entertainment, with huge audiences for Hollywood movies such as *Gone With the Wind*. Despite the war, the British film industry also carried on, producing work ranging from Laurence Olivier's *Henry V* to news and public information films and documentaries like Roy Boulting's *Desert Victory*, shot during the battle for El Alamein.

RIGHT: With the majority of young men in the forces, the young women at this open-air dance at Brockwell Park, London, partner each other.

BELOW: Shoppers and stallholders in Lambeth Walk carry on with 'business as usual' after a raid in the early days of the Blitz.

OPPOSITE PAGE ABOVE: Queuing for a special service at St Martin's Church.

OPPOSITE PAGE BELOW RIGHT: Chelsea pensioners wash crockery salvaged from the Royal Hospital after it was damaged in a raid.

OPPOSITE PAGE BELOW LEFT: Signs in Lambeth Walk point to the fact that this bomb-damaged thoroughfare is closed to traffic but shops are open for business.

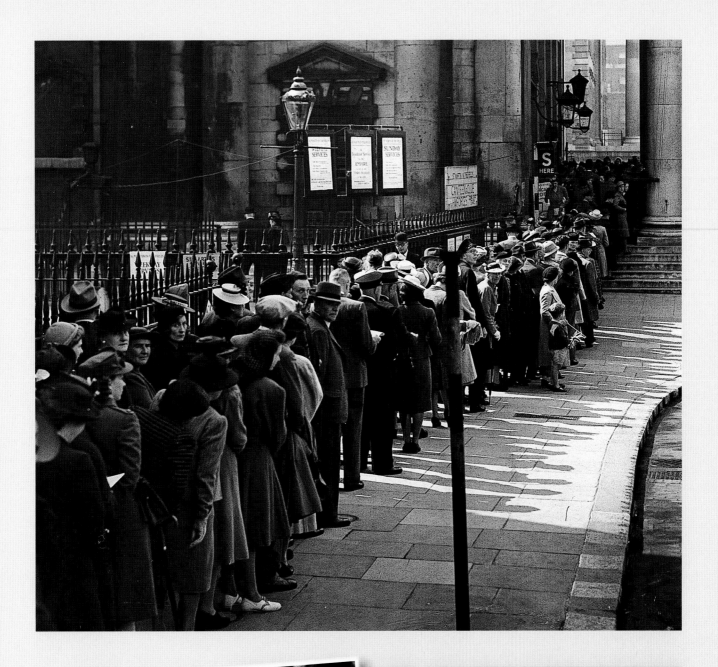

The BBC

It was as source of immense pride for the BBC that it never failed to transmit its programming throughout the war. As the only broadcaster at the time, the BBC carried the burden of providing both a reliable news service and morale-boosting entertainment. At the outbreak of war the company axed its embryonic television channel and all radio stations except for one. This single station was essential for morale during the war. Not only did the public feel they were getting a fair news picture, the BBC also broadcast programmes that became national institutions. Popular programmes, drawing millions of listeners, included *The Brains Trust*, *Woman's Hour*, *Children's Hour*, *Forces' Favourites*, and *Music While You Work*. However, the most popular programme was *ITMA (It's That Man Again)*, starring Tommy Handley. *ITMA* was a comedy sketch programme which made fun of everyone involved in the war, from Hitler to the Home Guard.

RIGHT TOP: Members of the Home Guard are rewarded with a concert, sponsored by the *Daily Mail*, at the Royal Albert Hall.

RIGHT MIDDLE: A close-up of the crowd at the Home Guard concert. While BBC Radio broadcast music on programmes such as *Forces' Favourites* and *Music While You Work*, live entertainment like this concert was rarer and much appreciated.

RIGHT BELOW: A Home Guard unit leaves a London cinema after a group outing.

Hope and prayer

ABOVE: On the fourth anniversary of the outbreak of war a National Day of Prayer was organised. This picture was taken at 11.00 a.m. in Trafalgar Square. The Church played a significant role in the war, organising such special services to cater for the country's spiritual needs, but also offering practical and social support through its various charitable organisations.

RIGHT: A meeting in Trafalgar Square in 1942 at which speakers from all political parties expressed their views on the importance of victory in that year.

LEFT: A Military Policeman takes over traffic duty in Whitehall, part of the increasing appearance of uniforms on the streets of Britain in the early weeks of the war.

BELOW: A roof spotter looks out for signs of an approaching raid while West Ham play Chelsea in December 1940, at the height of the Blitz. The gate was less than 2000.

BOTTOM RIGHT: Painting London tube signs with ultra-violet paint so that they could be read more easily in the blackout. The blackout changed the night-time landscape of Britain's towns and cities. It was the one thing that the majority of people said they found most inconvenient about the war.

BOTTOM LEFT: Illuminating the sign with ultra-violet light, which would not seem that different to the bluish blackout lights.

Football and the arts

Like many sports, the football programme was severely curtailed; many professional footballers were drafted into the army and although they could play as guest players for any club they chose when on leave from their unit, most teams were populated by teenage boys. In order to minimise travel, the leagues were reorganised by geographical area and by 1943 football gates were almost up to pre-war levels.

Although some theatres reopened a few weeks after the declaration of war, many actors were called up. Consequently, a full programme could not be sustained in the West End and many provincial and seaside theatres closed completely. However, some theatres and concert halls opened with a change of function – the Drury Lane Theatre was taken over by the forces' entertainment unit, ENSA, and the Royal Opera House was used as a dance hall.

Getting away from it all

ABOVE: August Bank Holiday, 1944, and this woman was determined to make the most of her day at the seaside. Even though by this stage of the war there was virtually no threat of an invasion, some coastal defences remained but bans on access to beaches began to be lifted.

RIGHT MIDDLE: Despite a government plea to stay at home for the August Bank Holiday in 1941, 'Paddington Station, as a result of petrol rationing, has more travellers than it could have expected before the war.'

RIGHT BELOW: Although almost 2000 yards of the beach had been cleared for access by the military during August 1944, at Angmering this is the closest these mothers and children can get to the sea.

In the open

ABOVE: 'Pictured in Charing Cross, a Canadian soldier gives a girl a buttonhole of spring primroses.'

RIGHT: It was difficult to obtain paper to print new books so libraries were very popular. Foyle's bookshop established an open-air library in what was formerly a refreshment kiosk in Hyde Park. Christina Foyle is pictured examining some of the books with a group of overseas soldiers.

OPPOSITE PAGE TOP: 'To overcome the telephonic and telegraphic difficulties in the City of London the Post Office today (11th January 1941) instituted a street telegram service. Messengers wearing appropriate notices parade in the streets within the vicinity of Northgate House and Regina House ready to receive telegrams.'

OPPOSITE PAGE BELOW RIGHT: After a raid, this gas man moves through the streets attending to damaged gas mains. He wears his tin helmet to protect him from falling masonry.

OPPOSITE PAGE BELOW LEFT: 'A newspaper seller in Fleet Street said people still wanted newspapers during the [air-raid] warnings and has supplied a tin hat for himself and stops at his post. His tin hat seems to give him security.'

Keeping the nation fed

Another strategy the government employed to promote the idea of a community spirit was the rationing system, which provided fair shares for all. It did not matter how rich you were, everyone got the same official ration. Additionally, prices of rationed and unrationed goods were strictly controlled to avoid profiteering. Apart from the capacity for the rich to buy more expensive, specially tailored clothing, it was generally not possible to buy something no one else could afford, unless it was purchased on the 'black market'. Even the Royal Family rationed themselves and stuck to the recommended five-inch-deep bath once a week to save fuel.

OPPOSITE PAGE TOP: This picture of a London street market during the first weeks of the war was published to promote the idea that there was no shortage of food and to try to prevent shortages occuring as a result of panic buying.

OPPOSITE PAGE BELOW LEFT: Queuing for a 'British Restaurant', a system of restaurants, each serving up to 500 meals a day, where for 1s 2d (6p) it was possible to buy a good-quality three-course meal. These meals were 'off the ration' and provided a valuable addition to the standard allocation, as well as saving customers valuable time, and fuel, by cooking their main meal of the day.

OPPOSITE PAGE BELOW RIGHT: The menu at a British Restaurant. This particular London restaurant extended its opening hours to serve hot meals to those, like firewatchers and ARP wardens, on duty at night.

BELOW INSET: Mrs Ramsey, a 72-year-old London resident, receives her 3501st cup of tea in Holborn tube station, where she frequently sheltered from air raids. In some of the larger shelters canteens serving hot meals were set up.

BELOW: A factory canteen. As the war progressed facilities for workers improved to include, in the larger factories, canteens serving hot food over and above the ration.

Making do

Everyone rose to the challenges of rationing and shortages. Creative ideas for cake recipes without eggs, fats, sugar; recipes to make meat and fish go further; recipes using food gathered from the wild; recipes for substitute foodstuffs, such as banana-flavoured parsnip as a sandwich filling, were shared by women. Everyone worked hard to 'make do and mend': children would be involved in unravelling old wool for re-use; men would mend old shoes and make toys and games for children; women would patch, sew and repair torn and old clothing. Most people, while often depressed by the shortages, took pride in their ingenuity and skill.

OPPOSITE PAGE TOP: Volunteers working with the Ministry of Food who served more than 12,000 meals to the people of Dover as they sheltered in these caves during periods of intense shelling from the French coast.

OPPOSITE PAGE BELOW: A communal centre on the coast of north-east England. These people, who were bombed out of their homes, are being fed at the centre, where they would stay until their houses could be repaired or new accommodation found.

RIGHT ABOVE: Baked potatoes on sale at Paddington Station as part of the 'Eat More Potatoes' campaign. Such food campaigns were spearheaded by Lord Woolton, the Minister of Food, and encouraged the avoidance of food waste and the consumption of unusual or plentiful foods.

RIGHT: Servicemen buy roast potatoes from a street seller in a port in the north of England. Potatoes were not rationed and provided a filling meal.

Relaxing in the sun

OPPOSITE PAGE: Knitting comfortably on a warm August day in Trafalgar Square as the air-raid siren wails.

OPPOSITE PAGE INSET: Shoppers carry on despite the sounding of an air-raid alert. Excuses were that it was 'too warm to take shelter' and that people were confident that the RAF would drive away the Luftwaffe bombers.

ABOVE: Londoners relax in the sunshine on the steps of St Martin-in-the-Fields during an air-raid warning in the last days of August 1940, just two weeks before the Blitz began.

RIGHT: Nurses from a mobile unit in north London relax with a game of football.

Fire of London

LEFT TOP AND MIDDLE: Workers walk to work past the fire tenders and burnt-out buildings on Monday, 30th December 1940, the morning after the raid that caused the second Fire of London.

BELOW: 'Outside their fire-wrecked office the staff of a City firm queue up to draw their weekly pay. A small table was the cashier's "office". On the ground lay a blackened typewriter – yesterday's glimpse of the "carry-on" City.'

OPPOSITE PAGE TOP: Following the fire Blitz on Sunday, 29th December 1940, soldiers help City clerks salvage books and files. The attack would create hours of painstaking work for the clerks as business records were checked and reconstituted.

OPPOSITE PAGE BELOW RIGHT: The Lord Mayor of London inspects books salvaged from the damaged Guildhall Library.

OPPOSITE PAGE BELOW LEFT: Workmen labour to provide a temporary roof to the Guildhall. Although the ancient walls remained relatively intact, the medieval building lost its roof in the fire.

Getting to work

ABOVE: On foot, by car or by bicycle, workers in a northern suburb of London head for their places of employment on Sunday, 26th May 1940, as they answer a call for a 'seven-day -a-week output effort'.

LEFT: As petrol rationing bites, City office workers hitch a lift with the few motorists who do have petrol for their cars.

OPPOSITE PAGE TOP: The Ministry of Transport instituted a new river boat service between Westminster and Woolwich. Petrol rationing meant the more public transport could be used the greater the saving and the more smoothly the capital would run.

OPPOSITE PAGE BELOW: Travellers could buy tickets on board the river boat service but people with 'tickets for the relative land journeys may use them'. The river boat service helped remove road congestion caused by Blitz debris and eased the strain on the bomb-damaged bus stock.

On the buses

LEFT: Buses such as as this one pictured in Fleet Street were brought in from the provinces to supplement London buses and to replace those lost during the Blitz.

BELOW LEFT: In October 1940, during the Blitz, London bus drivers and conductors were issued with tin helmets in recognition of the fact that they were frequently in danger when the bombing started.

BELOW RIGHT: This Manchester Corporation bus, drafted in to the London stock, is pictured in the process of having its destination roll changed.

OPPOSITE PAGE: As petrol rationing reduced the amount of vehicle fuel available, horse-drawn traffic, which by 1939 was a rarity on the streets of London, dramatically increased in number. Horses needed food for fuel but provided a good solution to the problem of delivering bulky or heavy loads.

Bus strike

OPPOSITE PAGE ABOVE: In response to a strike by London bus drivers, the government brought in the army. Here people board an army lorry in Hackney which substitutes for the regular bus service.

OPPOSITE PAGE BELOW: Women workers wait at the emergency service 'bus stop'.

LEFT: 'This one's full. The next one will be along in a minute.'

BELOW LEFT: Some soldiers drove buses. Here a London transport instructor gives directions to an army driver.

BELOW RIGHT: 'Pulling out into the traffic in Park Lane.'

CHAPTER NINE

Road to victory

The war is referred to as a 'world war' but for the first two years the conflict was largely confined to Europe, although Britain's position as a colonial power meant troops from the vast reaches of the British Empire served in her armies. When Italy declared war oN Britain on 10th June 1940, the war spread to North Africa. As part of the Axis Powers, Italy was intent on occupying land in North Africa as part of a plan to contol the Mediterranean; It already dominated the northern shore. The Eighth Army, the 'Desert Rats', led the attempt to keep the countries of North Africa free from Axis occupation. Britain and its allies had much to lose if Germany and Italy succeeded in commanding the southern shore of the Mediterranean; British-controlled areas such as Malta and Gibraltar would almost certainly fall into Axis hands.

By June the following year another fighting front had opened as Hitler, desperate for more resources, launched 'Operation Barbarossa', an attack on the USSR. In August 1939 Stalin had a non-aggression pact with Germany; many cite this as a principle reason why Germany felt secure enough to launch its invasion of Poland, the act that precipitated the war. Britain and Russia became allies, Churchill pledging British support to the Russian attempt to repel invading German forces. However, German blitzkrieg tactics proved useless in the USSR; the German Army found progress slow and battles in the harsh Russian winter conditions gruelling. Millions died in sieges of major Russian towns like Stalingrad (now Volgograd) and Leningrad (now St Petersburg).

In the early years, while Britain had stood largely alone, the USA had provided moral and practical support in the form of food and weapons. The Lend-Lease Agreement allowed Britain to obtain weapons and equipment without having to pay immediately – items were lent for the duration of the war, to be paid for after the war was won. Although President Roosevelt was sympathetic, there was no real appetite for America to commit troops to the fighting. That stance changed when the Japanese attacked the US naval base at Pearl Harbor, Hawaii, on 7th December 1941; another theatre of war opened, this time in the Pacific.

Thus, as 1942 commenced the conflict had engulfed much of the world. There was conflict in the Pacific, Russia and North Africa, as well as Europe where it had all started. The two sides were clearly drawn – the Allies: Britain, its colonies and those remnants of European countries that had managed to escape occupied Europe, the USSR and the USA; against them the Axis Powers: Germany, Italy and Japan. The road to victory was to be a slow and staged journey.

El Alamein to the fall of Italy

The first staging post on the road came with Italy's surrender on 8th September 1943, a victory made possible by the success of General Montgomery's Eighth Army at El Alamein in North Africa in November 1942. Britain allowed itself a brief moment of celebration and church bells, banned for the duration of the war as a signal of an invasion, rang throughout the land. Then the Eighth Army pressed on and in May 1943 110,000 German soldiers and 40,000 Italian soldiers surrendered. This brought an end to the North African campaign. Victory here secured a base from which to mount an assault on Italy, firstly taking the islands of Lampedusa, Pantelleria and Sicily before landing on the mainland and forcing the fall of Mussolini and the country's surrender.

OPPOSITE PAGE TOP: On 8th September 1943, news of Italy's surrender is chalked on a news vendor's board. After lightning strikes by the Allies, firstly on Sicily and then on the Italian mainland, Italy capitulated.

OPPOSITE PAGE BELOW: Reading the news of Italy's surrender, which was given by the anti-fascist Marshal Badoglio, who had replaced Mussolini, the fascist dictator, deposed soon after the Allies landed in Sicily in July 1943.

ABOVE: 6th June 1944 and people queue in the street for newspapers detailing the Allied invasion of mainland Europe. It was almost four years to the day since British troops had retreated from the beaches at Dunkirk in Normandy.

LEFT: A French Tricolor is hung out in Soho by French exiles to celebrate the fall of Paris on 24th August 1944. Following the D Day landings and fierce battles in Normandy, the Allies moved swiftly through France to recapture Paris.

Allied assaults

For the Allies 1944 was a vital year in the journey to victory. In January, American forces landed at Anzio to attack the German troops occupying northern Italy, despite the Rome government's surrender to the Allies. Further east, in the USSR, the Red Army began to gain the upper hand against Hitler's troops, pushing them westward towards Germany. But the most significant assault of the year was the long-awaited D Day Landings in June in which the Allies attacked the northern coast of Normandy; Success here enabled a push which forced the German Army back towards Germany. Later that same year, in October, General MacArthur, heading a force of a quarter of a million men, re-took the Philippines as the beginning of an all-out assault on the Japanese military in the Pacific.

OPPOSITE PAGE TOP: September 1944. 'Confidence for sale. The Oxford-street barrow man thinks victory is just around the corner. He knows he will find customers of the same mind.'

OPPOSITE PAGE MIDDLE: As the lanscape gets 'back to normal, the protective covering around Eros is removed.

OPPOSITE PAGE BELOW: Although dated 2nd May 1945, this proclamation makes clear the conviction that an Allied victory in Europe is a certainty.

RIGHT: These workmen are replacing the globes on the street lights in Piccadilly, ready for a return to normal lighting.

BELOW: A Soho bar where French patriots and the British celebrate the fall of Paris. Despite the celebrations in London and the progress of the Allies in France, London and the south-east had become prey to the pilotless bombs – the V1 flying bombs, nicknamed buzzbombs or doodlebugs – and the V2 rocket bombs.

German surrender

From France in the west, from Russia in the east and from Italy and Greece in the south, German troops were pushed back into home territory throughout 1944 and into 1945. German towns and cities suffered some of the most devastating air raids of the war; thousands were killed, but the destruction of weapons production and infrastructure enabled the Allies to secure the upper hand. Last-ditch efforts in the Battle of the Bulge and attempts to attack Britain with the new pilotless bombs, the V1s and V2s, were not enough for Germany to wrest the initiative. In the face of defeat and as the Red Army took control in the ruined streets of Berlin, Hitler committed suicide on 30th April 1945. Field Marshal Keitel signed Germany's unconditional surrender on 8th May and the victory and peace in Europe was secure.

ABOVE: Crowds meet in Piccadilly Circus to hear the news of the final surrender of Nazi Germany.

RIGHT: On 8th May 1945, crowds wait patiently in Whitehall for the official announcement that 'This is VE Day'.

OPPOSITE PAGE TOP: 7th May 1945 and people gather outside Downing Street, spilling into Whitehall as they wait for news of Germany's final surrender. Although German troops had surrendered following Hitler's suicide on 30th April, the final signature on a declaration of unconditional surrender was not yet forthcoming.

OPPOSITE PAGE MIDDLE: 8th May and crowds line Parliament Street waiting for Winston Churchill's announcement from the balcony of the Ministry of Health and the commencement of VE Day celebrations.

OPPOSITE PAGE BELOW: As the celebrations gather momentum the Australian flag is carried. Although fighting continued in the Pacific, VE Day was a time of joy for all the Allied nations.

Peace in Europe

Although the peace began officially at one minute past midnight on 9th May 1945, the celebrations started on Tuesday, 8th May and went on throughout the night. The entire country celebrated in the streets, but London was the focus of the biggest festivities. Crowds had gathered in Whitehall, waiting for an official announcement of peace in Europe. The announcement was expected at 9.00 a.m. on the 8th May but it was not until 3.00 p.m. that Prime Minister Winston Churchill broadcast to the nation, the news relayed through loudspeakers in the centre of London. He said that the war in Europe would end at midnight, and praised the British people and their allies, but he also reminded them that Japan was not yet defeated.

OPPOSITE: Silence in Trafalgar Square as the crowds listen to the relay of Prime Minister Winston Churchill's broadcast announcing the official end to war with Germany and a public holiday – VE Day.

OPPOSITE PAGE TOP: Westminster is thronged with people, just some of of the 50,000 who celebrated in London on VE Day.

OPPOSITE PAGE BOTTOM: Crowds bring traffic to a standstill in Piccadilly Circus.

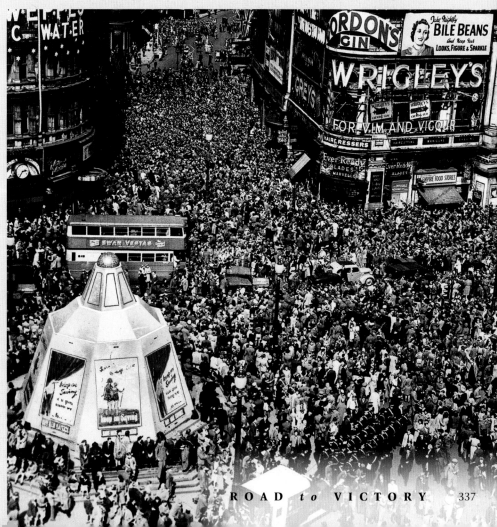

Celebrations

Churchill's broadcast was the signal for the party to begin throughout Britain. In central London around 50,000 revellers thronged the streets, many making their way to Buckingham Palace, calling for the King and Queen who, with their daughters, Princesses Elizabeth and Margaret, and Winston Churchill, appeared eight times on the royal balcony to acknowledge the crowds' joy. Celebrations continued as darkness fell and licensing laws were suspended for the night. Although everyone knew that the war was not over and the war in the Pacific continued, there was unrestrained joy after more than five and a half years of danger, deprivation and loss. The following Sunday, attendance at prayers of thanksgiving throughout Britain was so great that in many churches the services had to be relayed by loudspeaker to those outside.

ABOVE: ATS and American soldiers cheer from one of the plinths in Trafalgar Square.

BELOW: 8th May 1945 was a warm sunny day, reflecting the mood of the nation, and this group was one of many to paddle in the Trafalgar Square fountains.

OPPOSITE PAGE: In Piccadilly Circus, adventurous revellers climb the protective shell around the statue of Eros.

Gathering at Buckingham Palace

ABOVE: The King, Queen, Churchill and the Princesses Elizabeth and Margaret appeared on the royal balcony eight times to acknowledge the crowds. Later on in the evening, princesses left the Palace to join the revellers in the streets.

RIGHT: In the Mall the crowds call for the King to appear on the Palace balcony. The Royal Family had remained in the Palace throughout the war, refusing evacuation to a safer area, a gesture that was much appreciated by the nation.

OPPOSITE PAGE ABOVE: A sea of people outside Buckingham Palace on VE Day.

OPPOSITE PAGE BELOW: A cheer goes up for the King, Queen and the Princesses Elizabeth and Margaret as they appear on the balcony. Later Prime Minister Churchill joined them.

Lighting up the night

LEFT: Churchill, members of the Cabinet and the Chiefs of Staff with the King at Buckingham Palace, which became the centre for much of the celebrations during the daylight hours.

BELOW: On VE Day, Winston Churchill walks with other MPs to St Margaret's Church for a service of thanksgiving, as mounted police hold back the crowds of well-wishers.

BELOW INSET: Admiralty Arch floodlit on the night of VE Day. After the focus on the Palace during the day, the revellers moved down the Mall, joining with others in Piccadilly, where licensing laws had been suspended for the night.

OPPOSITE PAGE: Floodlights illuminate the cross on top of St Paul's Cathedral.

Street party!

MAIN PICTURE: At this street party in Hunslet, Leeds, national flags provide the bunting and a victory sign is chalked on the cobbles as the residents gather to celebrate.

OPPOSITE PAGE INSET: The residents of Kentwell Close in Brockley, south London, organised this children's party on VE Day.

BELOW: 'Street tea parties celebrate "V" Whitsun. Not everybody went from London to the seaside and other places this Whitsun (21st May 1945). Some preferred to stay at home like these residents of Tilloch Street, Islington, who organised tea parties in the street for the children, complete with paper hats and decorations.'

A final end to the war

Despite the joys of VE Day, the final end to the war was not to come for another three months as the war in the Pacific raged on. The Japanese surrender came only after the dropping of two atomic bombs. The first fell on Hiroshima on 6th August 1945; three days later, a second destroyed Japan's shipbuilding centre of Nagasaki. It took further days of negotiation before the official surrender on 14th August 1945 and the end of the Second World War. For the population of Britain the war had lasted twenty days short of six years.

News of the Japanese surrender was broadcast in Britain by the new Prime Minister, Clement Attlee; his announcement was made at midnight on the 14th. The sleeping population was wakened by the sounds of ships' sirens and train whistles. People rose and gathered in streets throughout Britain, lighting specially prepared bonfires, setting off flares and fireworks. By 3.00 a.m. the crowds in Piccadilly were as large as those on VE Day. The 15th and 16th of August were designated as V Day public holidays, as the nation celebrated and offered prayers of thanksgiving before it turned to face the peace.

OPPOSITE PAGE: Crowds line the streets around St Paul's on Sunday, 13th May 1945 as the King and Queen leave the cathedral after a service of thanksgiving for the peace in Europe and prayers for a swift final end to the war.

OPPOSITE PAGE INSET: The scene in Piccadilly Circus at 3.00 a.m. on VJ Day.

BELOW TOP: On Sunday, 19th August churches were full and overflow services were held outside many churches. Here people pray outside St Martin-in-the-Fields.

BELOW BOTTOM: The Aldwych on 11th August 1945, 'snowed up' by a rain of paper thrown from offices along its length following news of the defeat of Japan.

Demob happy

ABOVE: After the war ended millions of men had to be demobilised and the British military aimed to complete the paperwork for each man in 10 minutes; it was essential to avoid a backlog in order to make the return to 'Civvy Street' as smooth as possible. Here an ex-soldier tries on one of the millions of off-the-peg suits produced for demobbed men to prepare them for their peacetime roles.

ABOVE INSET: Advice was available to the soldier returning to 'Civvy Street'. Here advice is offered on that most important fashion accessory of the period – a hat.

OPPOSITE PAGE TOP LEFT: A 'Civvy Clothing Shop' was held at Olympia for demobbed soldiers. Here a soldier tries on a civilian suit jacket.

OPPOSITE PAGE RIGHT: Being measured for a demob suit. Many men had been in service for the duration and had not had new civilian clothing for years. Their clothing entitlement is outlined on the sign.

OPPOSITE PAGE BELOW RIGHT: Private H. Salter, being measured here, is the first man to claim a 'non-austerity discharge suit'. Austerity Regulations had come into effect in March 1942. Clothing styles which used valuable materials merely for show were not permitted; so double-breasted jackets, turn-ups on trousers and decorative buttons were banned. By the time Private Salter was ready for discharge in October 1944, the war was going well enough for the regulations to be relaxed.

OPPOSITE PAGE BELOW LEFT: Here is a happy Private Salter with his complete demob outfit.

OPPOSITE PAGE MIDDLE LEFT: A soldier is issued with pay, ration books, identity cards and health card, all part of the paperwork that was needed for life outside the military.

AND AWAIT
TO BE MEASURED

YOU ARE ENTITLED T.O

1 SUIT.   1 TIE.
1 RAINCOAT.   1 HAT.
1 SHIRT.   1 PR SHOES.
2 COLLARS.   2 PRS SOCKS.

YOU WILL SERVE
YOURSELF.
CIVILIAN EXPERTS ARE
RE TO ASSIST YOU.

Peacetime

Fifty-five million of the world's citizens had lost their lives in the conflict and throughout Europe the long process of reconstruction began. Britain faced years of austerity as it worked to pay the financial costs of the war. The nation had to turn its economy and industry from a single-minded focus on the war effort to more diverse peacetime production. However, it took time; rationing continued for a further nine years, indeed in some instances became more severe – bread was rationed even though it never had been during wartime.

As millions of men and women were demobilised from the armed forces and evacuees returned home, families and communities had to learn to live together in peacetime social structures that were, in many ways, very different to those in existence before 3rd September 1939.

OPPOSITE PAGE TOP: 'Battle signatures' at a reunion of pilots from Biggin Hill in September 1946 at the White Hart Hotel at Brasted in Kent, which served as the flyers' unofficial headquarters during the war.

OPPOSITE PAGE BELOW The secret Operations Room in the underground War Cabinet Rooms beneath Storey's Gate. The pins on the map on the wall mark the position of ships and men when the war ended. On 16th August 1945 the lights were switched off for the first time since the shelter had come into commission in mid-1940 and the door was locked. In 1948 Parliament announced that the site was to be preserved, but until 1981 access was restricted. The complex has now been preserved and restored. It is open to the public to give people an impression of what life was like for those in charge of the conduct of the war.

BELOW RIGHT: The Operations Room from where Churchill broadcast many of his stirring war speeches.

BELOW LEFT: Churchill's desk in Storey's Gate. The underground shelter covered six acres, housing 200 rooms, 40 feet below ground and protected by 17-foot thick reinforced concrete.

ACKNOWLEDGEMENTS

The photographs in this book are from the archives of the Daily Mail.
That this book can be published is a tribute to the dedication of the staff, past
and present, in the Picture Library at Associated Newspapers.
Particular thanks to Steve Torrington, Alan Pinnock, Dave Sheppard,
Brian Jackson, Paul Rossiter and all the staff.

Thanks also to
Gordon Mills, Mark Brown, John Dunne, Cliff Salter, Richard Betts, Peter Wright,
Trevor Bunting, Vicki Harris, Simon Taylor and Frances Hill.

Bibliography

The People's War by Angus Calder, pub: Panther

How We Lived Then by Norman Longmate, pub: Hutchinson

Living Through the Blitz by Tom Harrisson, pub: Penguin

Children of the Blitz by Robert Westall, pub: Macmillan

The Blitz Then and Now (2 Volumes) ed. Winston Ramsay, pub: After the Battle Publications

Blitz on Britain 1939–1945 by Alfred Price, pub: Sutton Publications

Bombers and Mash by Raynes Minn, pub: Virago

War Papers introduced by Ludovic Kennedy, pub: Collins

Life on the Home Front by Tim Healey, pub: Readers Digest

Chronicle of the Twentieth Century edited by Derrick Mercer pub: Longman